To Zululand with the R.E.

To Zululand with the R.E.
The Recollections of Two Officers of the Royal Engineers During the Anglo-Zulu War, 1879

ILLUSTRATED

Zulu War Experiences

by Sir Richard Harrison, Sir Bindon Blood

and

The Services of Royal Engineers During the Zulu War, 1879

(An Extract from 'The History of the Royal Engineers')

Whitworth Porter

To Zululand with the R.E.
*The Recollections of Two Officers of the Royal Engineers
During the Anglo-Zulu War, 1879*
Zulu War Experiences
by Sir Richard Harrison, Sir Bindon Blood
and
*The Services of Royal Engineers During the Zulu War, 1879
(An Extract from 'The History of the Royal Engineers')*
by Whitworth Porter

ILLUSTRATED

FIRST EDITION IN THIS FORM

Extracts first published in the titles
Recollections of a Life in the British Army
Four Score Years and Ten
and
The History of the Royal Engineers

Leonaur is an imprint of Oakpast Ltd
Copyright in this form © 2023 Oakpast Ltd

ISBN: 978-1-916535-34-3 (hardcover)
ISBN: 978-1-916535-35-0 (softcover)

http://www.leonaur.com

Publisher's Notes
The views expressed in this book are not necessarily
those of the publisher.

Contents

Zulu War Experiences   7
By Sir Richard Harrison

Zulu War Experiences   95
By Sir Bindon Blood

The Services of Royal Engineers During the Zulu War, 1879
(An extract from *The History of the Royal Engineers*)   131
By Whitworth Porter

Sir Richard Harrison

Zulu War Experiences
By Sir Richard Harrison

On February 11, 1879, news reached England of a terrible disaster at the Cape. A British column consisting of a wing of the 24th Foot, some native levies and others were annihilated by the Zulus on January 21, 500 men and about forty officers being killed. The next day orders were received at Aldershot to prepare certain regiments of cavalry and infantry, &c., to go out at once, and I received notice to hold myself in readiness to go to Chatham, and take command of the 30th Field Company, R.E., which had been ordered to concentrate there.

Many a time have the people of England been startled by the accounts received from some seat of war; but never, I think, has such a shock been felt at home as when the morning papers proclaimed that an organised British force had been almost annihilated by the badly armed though brave warriors of the Kaffir king, Ketchwayo, on the borders of Zululand.

The news of this catastrophe arrived at Aldershot on February 11, 1879. The next day several regiments at that station, and a good many individual officers, received orders to hold themselves in readiness to proceed to the Cape at short notice. I was among the number, my command being a Field Company, R.E., which was to be raised at Chatham, and then sent to Aldershot to be prepared for the approaching campaign.

At that time no complete system of mobilisation existed in our army—all making up of units to war strength, all equipment, all organisation, including the appointment of generals

24th Foot in South Africa

and staff, had to be elaborated on the spur of the moment. Thus, my company had to be made up from others that were remaining at home—only one officer and some twenty men of the old company remained with it, all the other officers, sergeants, and rank and file, having to be taken from elsewhere; and every man had to be equipped, specially clothed, and his accounts adjusted before we started. Then we had to get horses, and harness, wagons, and special engineer stores, some of the patterns of which were not yet settled; and all this had to be accomplished with the greatest rapidity, because the day and hour of our embarkation was an uncertain quantity.

Then, too, private affairs had to be arranged; where my wife and children were to live, what servants we should keep, what horses we must sell. Finally, my own kit and clothing for the war had to be looked up and bought. So, there was not much time to think, and I put off, until we got on board ship, any consideration regarding the work on which we might be employed when we landed, or whether any improvements might be made in organisation and equipment, to enable us the better to face the special circumstances of the war.

The weather was extremely cold at this time, snow lay all over the roads and was piled up between the huts.

On February 17 my company, numbering about two hundred men, arrived at Aldershot from Chatham; and the next day we were paraded for inspection by the Commander-in-Chief, H.R.H. the Duke of Cambridge. I had been officially transferred to the company that morning from the Pontoon troop. I was then a regimental major and brevet lieutenant-colonel, and I became a full colonel soon after our arrival at the Cape. The other officers were Captain B. Blood (who has since distinguished himself very much in India), Lieut. Sherrard, Lieut. McKeen, and Lieut. Littledale. We had nearly all the men on parade, and six of our wagons, though not all our stores.

The commander-in-chief complimented us on our appearance, but did not examine our stores. On asking, as usual, if there were 'any complaints,' I replied that 'I thought under the circumstances of the campaign, the drivers should be supplied with a pistol or some arm, in case they were detached and fell in with any stray Zulus.' My remark caused some excitement among the Headquarter Staff, but it had its effect, and the arms I asked for were issued.

Having sent an advanced party to Portsmouth, and packed our wagons and heavy baggage on railway trucks the previous evening, on February 27 we left Aldershot for the war.

My journal for that day is as follows:

> Company marched at 7.45 in a snowstorm. Train from Aldershot at 9.0. Beached Portsmouth about 11.30, and got all on board the *Palmyra* by 2.30. Horses unharnessed on shore, and slung on to the main deck. Men marched to their messes (eight in a mess). Wagons unpacked, and all taken to pieces and carried on board. Men quiet and well behaved, not one the least the worse for drink, no absentees, and no equipment left behind. At 3.0 we steamed away.

As senior army officer I commanded the troops on board and made Captain Blood adjutant. As soon as I had issued the necessary orders for the routine on board ship, I set to work to consider the position at the Cape, and make such notes as I thought might be useful for the approaching campaign. I will state very briefly what that position was, and then we will get back to the voyage.

Not many years ago the Zulus were one of a number of pastoral tribes spread over the country now occupied by Natal and Kaffirland. Without going into their history, or that of the Dutch settlers with whom they were frequently in conflict, it will be enough for our present purpose to say that, under the leadership first of Chaka and afterwards of his brother Dingaan, they became one of the best organised African native tribes of the nineteenth century. All the young men in the community had to be soldiers and were concentrated for several months in the year, at the will of the king, in one or other of the large military *kraals* that he possessed.

There they were trained in the arts of war, and there they were assembled whenever the king wished to make an expedition against some tribe that had offended him. None of these young soldiers were allowed to marry without his permission; but this was usually given after a successful raid at which they had, as it was called, 'washed their spears.' Even after their marriage, however, they were held available for use in war, if specially required. It was the custom in the country for the women to do all the work, even that of building the huts in which they lived, the men doing very little more than hunting and fighting.

Besides the extraordinary hold that this system gave to the king over the fighting power of the nation, the material, *i.e.*, the trained soldier, was exceptionally good, and the tactics they employed were well suited to the warfare in which they usually engaged. The Zulus have been described as lithe and active, well-knit, and capable of great endurance. My own experience of them bears this out. A young Zulu chief, who had been attached to the intelligence department of our army, and joined me the evening of the Battle of Ulundi, afforded me a good opportunity of observing the characteristics of the fine race to which he belonged. I will tell more about him later on. Meantime I will confine myself to saying that he never seemed to tire. Only give him a gun and a few cartridges to carry, and he would follow you all day, even if you had a change of two or three horses, and he seemed just as fresh at the end of a long march as he was at the start.

The well-known tactics of the Zulus consisted of an attack with a central body, and two wings (or horns). When advancing, previous to an attack, they formed in a snake-like column, which wound its way through hill and valley, keeping concealed as much as possible. Then when they arrived at what their leaders considered the striking point, they deployed very rapidly, and endeavoured with their 'horns' to sweep round both flanks of the enemy, and, if possible, surround him.

In early days their weapons were two or three javelins, or

ZULU WARRIORS

throwing *assegais*, a stabbing *assegai*, and a shield; but of late years rifles, when they could be procured, took the place of the throwing *assegais*. In skirmishing they acted very much in the same way as they did in the attack by large bodies, always trying with a few men to turn your flank, while others came straight at you; but, until they actually charged, they took every advantage of ground to conceal their advance.

I can give an instance from my own experience of their skill and rapidity in utilising ground. During the advance against Ulundi, it became necessary to reconnoitre some rough wooded hills that lay across our path. It was thought probable that these hills would be held by Zulus; how strongly no one could say. Evidently it was advisable to be prepared for any contingency. The reconnaissance was entrusted to Major-General Marshall, the leader of the Cavalry Brigade. Colonel Buller, of Wood's Column, with his Irregular Horse, were to be at that General's disposal for the day. I was to go out independently with my own escort to see what happened and report to the commander-in-chief.

Starting in good time I found Buller engaged with some Zulus at the foot of the hills. Eventually he drove them back into the rocks and bush that covered the hillside, and then he directed his men to feed their horses and cook their coffee, so as to be ready for further action. I did the same, my little bivouac being on the flank of the one occupied by the Irregulars, but, owing to a depression in the ground, not in view of it. While I was sitting on a rock, looking at the position with my field-glasses, Buller came over from his bivouac to talk to me. I pointed out to him some Zulus creeping down into a *donga* about 1,000 yards from where we were sitting, and said 'From your experience of Zulu fighting, how long would it take those men to get to us if they wanted to attack?'

He replied 'Ten minutes,' and then he went away. I ordered the horses to be saddled, but I did not stop the cooking of the coffee, because it was nearly ready, and I thought there was quite time enough to issue it to the men before we moved. I should add that there was no apparent 'cover' for men between the place where I saw the Zulus and our bivouac. But, by the watch I held in my hand, not five minutes had gone before a volley was fired at us from what looked like a few tufts of grass 200 to 300 yards off. This disconcerted my cooks and they spilt the coffee. My escort then retired as usual by alternate wings, firing as they went, and the Zulu advance at this point was checked until Marshall and the Regulars arrived. We suffered nothing more than the loss of our breakfast.

It is obvious that troops such as I have described must have certain advantages over the slow-moving, cumbersome forces that form the fighting strength of European nations. The Zulu Warrior could move as quickly and as far as cavalry, and at the same time conceal himself in folds of the ground as readily as Infantry; he required no transport except a few women and boys to carry his simple food, and these advanced as quickly as he did; and so a Zulu Army could march forty or fifty miles in any direction, and then fight a battle.

But, at the same time, it is obvious that as a fighting force they had their weaknesses. They had no artillery; they were indifferent shots with a rifle, and never, I believe, used a bayonet. Throughout the Zulu War the rifle was used by them only as a secondary weapon in place of a throwing *assegai*; and, as often as not, it was thrown away when the charge took place, to enable the stabbing *assegai* to be used with a freer arm and more deadly effect.

Then they could not carry on any prolonged campaign. Assembled at one of the king's *kraals*, by a message from village to village, to be 'doctored,' *i.e.*, put through a certain superstitious ceremonial, under the direction of one or other of the royal chiefs, they were formed into an '*impi*' or fighting force, and then sent on the raid for which they were called together. The raid over, whether successful or not, the '*impi*' broke up, and the warriors dispersed to their villages, and, if further operations were required, another assembly had to be made.

Similar arrangements were carried out, on a smaller scale,

by chiefs at a distance from the royal *kraal*, when it was so ordered by the king; and besides these '*impis*,' the warriors of a village would, without having been 'doctored,' make attacks on small parties known to be hostile. It was not difficult to find out whether or not '*impis*' were being formed and to take such precautions against their attack as were necessary; while against minor attacks by a few villagers you had to be always prepared day and night.

Evidently it was for us—British officers—in conducting a war against the Zulus to consider all the advantages and disadvantages of their system, and to frame our own plans accordingly. So, on the voyage to the Cape, I not only read the history of what had taken place in South Africa since white men had first landed in the country, but also studied the nature and peculiarities of each race existing on the soil, and tried to make up my mind what would be likely to happen when the troops I had the honour to command put foot on shore, and how I could help them to do all that was possible to carry out to the full any duty that they might be required to perform.

The result of my cogitations I communicated to my men in the shape of standing orders, which I will not recapitulate here—they are dry reading even to those concerned; but I may say that in those standing orders I endeavoured to convey to those who read them, in as concise and clear a manner as possible, what were the peculiar dangers of the war, and how they could best be guarded against.

Before returning to my own personal narrative, I will tell you very shortly what was the position at the Cape when we left England to go there.

The Governor of Cape Colony, who was also the High Commissioner in South Africa, was Sir Bartle Frere; the General commanding the troops was Lord Chelmsford; the Governor of Natal was Sir Edward Bulwer; and the Administrator of the Transvaal was Sir Owen Lanyon. After some experience with the Kaffirs in Cape Colony, Sir Bartle Frere had come to the conclusion that the country would never settle down as long as

Ketchwayo, the new king in Zululand, continued in power.

The Zulus had had a quiet time under the rule of Impanda, the youngest brother of Dingaan and Chaka; but when Impanda died and was succeeded by his son Ketchwayo, it soon became evident that the young king had every intention of following in the steps of his uncles rather than in those of his father. When, in September 1873, Sir Theophilus Shepstone, the clever Minister for Native Affairs in Natal, attended by request the installation of Ketchwayo as ruler of the Zulu people, the entire assembly agreed that indiscriminate shedding of blood should cease. But not many months after the new ruler was placed on the throne, the Governor of Natal had to complain that, in a fit of savage caprice, he had ordered the slaughter of some girls who had endeavoured to elude his fiat that they should be married to the soldiers of one of his old regiments. To this complaint the king replied:

> I do kill, but do not consider yet I have done anything in the way of killing. Why do the white people start at nothing? I have not yet begun; I have yet to kill; it is the custom of our nation, and I shall not depart from it.

The immediate cause of the war was a violation of British territory. Two Zulu women in some sudden terror fled across the border into Natal. They were pursued by an armed band, and forcibly taken back in face of a party of Natal native police, and it is believed killed. The Governor of Natal, and later the High Commissioner, demanded that the leaders of the raid should be given up and put on their trial in a court of law, and if this requirement was not complied with within thirty days, the general commanding the British forces would be instructed to compel compliance. No satisfactory reply was made to this intimation, and on January 11, 1879, the British troops crossed the frontier into Zululand.

If the reader will look at a map of South Africa, he will see that, eastward of the British Colony of Natal, and divided from it by a river that in its lower reaches is called the Tugela, lies

Zululand. Speaking roughly, it is a square, with sides of about one hundred miles; and almost in its centre are situated Ketchwayo's great military *kraals*, known by the name of Ulundi. Lord Chelmsford's plan of campaign was to advance simultaneously from west and north towards these *kraals*.

In order to carry this out he formed three columns operating from Natal, *viz.* one under Colonel Pearson near the mouth of the Tugela, one under Colonel Glyn near Rorke's Drift, and one under Colonel Durnford about halfway between the other two. Then there was a fourth column, operating from Utrecht, under Brigadier-General E. Wood; and a fifth in the Transvaal, keeping in check a great chief called Sekukuni, a friend and ally of Ketchwayo's, whose stronghold was in the Lulu Mountains near Lydenburg.

The campaign commenced by the advance of Glyn's column, which pitched its tents at Isandlwana, not far over the frontier. The commander-in-chief of the army (Lord Chelmsford) accompanied this column, and on the morning of January 22 left the camp in charge of six companies of the 24th Regiment, two guns, and some eight hundred native troops; and, having sent for Colonel Durnford, with the mounted troops of his column, to join them, went forward with the rest of the force to reconnoitre and choose the road for a further advance. But what happened? While he was away following some Zulus, who fell back slowly before his troops, the main body of the enemy poured down on the camp.

An excellent little book, describing the Zulu system and the Zulu tactics, had been brought out by the British Staff in South Africa, and distributed before the campaign; but the special lessons therein inculcated were either distrusted or forgotten. Anyhow, the camp was not prepared for defence; the troops were not kept together, and there was no concerted plan of action. The result was the complete destruction of the force that Lord Chelmsford had left behind to guard his line of communication at the Isandlwana camp.

Fortunately for the safety of Natal, a small post at Rorke's

Drift, which had been hastily fortified by Chard of the Engineers and Bromhead of the 24th, sufficed to stop the Zulus after their victory at Isandlwana. So, the warriors broke up and returned to their villages, and, when Glyn's column returned in the evening, they found nothing but the bodies of their comrades and other signs of the hard-fought battle.

The result of this first engagement of the Zulu War was to bring out from England the reinforcements of which my field company of Royal Engineers formed a part. While we were on our way, the British columns did not continue their advance into Zululand, but strengthened themselves in their various positions, and made such preparation as was possible for the combined advance, whenever it might take place. I will now return to our voyage.

As I have before said, we left Portsmouth Harbour on the afternoon of February 27 for the Cape. Our transport was one of the smaller vessels of the Cunard line, called the *Palmyra*, which steamed about twelve knots an hour.

On the night of March 4, we passed Madeira, and on the 8th, we reached St. Vincent, where we had to stop and coal. Here we found five transports in the harbour, waiting to coal, *viz.* the *Russia* with the 58th Regiment on board, the *England* and the *France* with the 17th Lancers, and the *Egypt* and the *Spain* with the King's Dragoon Guards. The coal was brought alongside in lighters, and, the amount of procurable labour being very limited, the process of supply was a tedious one. It is a matter for reflection how far, in a country like ours which is governed by *party*, the actual government of the day should be held responsible for the conduct of naval and military operations.

I cannot help hoping that the Council of Imperial Defence, which has lately been put on a more or less permanent footing, may define that responsibility. Surely the misfortune that befell our arms in South Africa was not the fault of the government that happened to be in power at the time. Consequently, it should not have been thought necessary, in order to ease their shoulders from blame, to send reinforcements to the seat of war

Chard with medal and other Royal Engineers

before the whole matter had been properly thought out, and full preparations made.

In order to show how quickly an expedition could be sent from England, even to so distant a colony as the Cape, the transports that left our shores were loaded anyhow, and sent to coal at a place where the supply was limited, where all the water had to be condensed, and where all fruit, vegetables, and meat had to be imported. The *Russia* had all her army stores pitched on board helter-skelter, and shied into the hold anyhow by the numerous dockyard hands supplied for the purpose at Portsmouth; and when she got to sea it was discovered that the things required on the voyage were at the bottom of the hold, and the troops had to be supplied from the officers' stock of provisions until their own stores were got up.

The *Palmyra* (our ship) was laden with 800 tons less cargo than she could have carried, which made her too light to steam well in the trade winds. If she had been filled up, even with coal, we should have saved several days of time and a considerable quantity of money.

Among the officers on board the transports that we found at St. Vincent there were no fewer than four generals: Marshall, commanding the Cavalry; E. Newdigate and Crealock, sent out to command divisions; and Clifford, commanding the communications, a new appointment in our army, but a very necessary one. I had known all these officers in England, especially at Aldershot, where I used frequently to be employed in Staff duties; and while we were waiting, I went round and paid them all visits. As it was thought that the Engineers were wanted at the front as soon as anyone, and the *Palmyra* only required a small supply, we were allowed to coal out of our turn, and got away soon after midday on the 9th. On the 27th we arrived at Simon's Bay, and I reported to Captain Adeane, R.N., the senior naval officer.

We were told that the cavalry transports were to coal at Table Bay, and the infantry ones at Simon's Bay, and then all go on to Durban. The only orders we received were 'to land heavy baggage.' No one knew what this meant, whether it included men's bags. I interpreted it as not doing so, and, having given the men what boots and clothes they wanted for the campaign, ordered the rest of the clothing and any spare officers' baggage to be sent on shore.

The only war news we received was that a convoy of the 80th Regiment had been destroyed by a Zulu '*impi*' in the vicinity of Luneberg, and that a force had been collected to relieve Colonel Pearson's column, which had been shut up for some weeks in a fort at Etshowe. At the same time, we heard more details about the Isandlwana fight. It appears that some 900 Europeans and as many native troops on our side were killed. (The actual figure was somewhat higher with 52 officers, 727 British regulars and 476 Colonial and Native troops killed. In total 1,300.) It is understood that Colonel Durnford arrived in camp about half an hour before the Zulus appeared, and went out at once with his mounted men to attack them.

Colonel Pulleine supported him with the infantry, and formed his men up in line in front of the camp. The camp was not in any way prepared for defence, and no guards or reserves were left in it. The Zulus attacked as usual in front and on both flanks (just as described in Lord Chelmsford's book), and, sweeping round, came through the camp and on to the rear of Colonel Pulleine's fighting line, after which the affair was over in a few minutes.

Although I am not giving the history of this battle, I cannot refrain from mentioning the dauntless courage of Durnford and the Natal Horse at this juncture. Arriving at Isandlwana, with his mounted men, soon after Lord Chelmsford had left it, Colonel Durnford, in a short conversation with Pulleine, 24th Regiment, the officer in local command, explained that he would at once advance against the Zulus, in order to find out what they were doing, and then, if necessary, he would fall back on the camp.

But, on going out as arranged, he discovered that the Zulu force in the immediate neighbourhood was much greater than he had anticipated. It was with some difficulty that he could even for a time hold in check that portion of the army (the central body) that he found in front of him. He did not cover sufficient ground to have any influence at all on the two wings (or horns) that were being pushed forward by the Zulu leaders, to carry out their usual tactics of surrounding their enemy.

Under these circumstances he fell back slowly, by alternate squadrons, holding on as long as possible to each position occupied, and causing considerable loss by his fire to the brave savages who were attacking him. On arriving at the neck of land that connects Isandlwana Hill with the low range to the southward, Durnford saw that the Zulu horns had got in rear of the camp. A scattered fight was in progress all over the plain, and a crowd of fugitives, chiefly Natal natives, were streaming away, in an endeavour to cross the river and get into Natal. He came to the conclusion that the only chance of saving any of those who were thus trying to escape, if not of retrieving the day, was to endeavour with a disciplined force to hold the neck.

So, he formed up and addressed his troopers, explaining the situation, and stating that he himself intended to stop on the neck. To a man, I believe, these horsemen from Natal caught their leader's enthusiasm. They had already done a good day's work; they could, without fear of blame, have ridden off, and given the alarm at Rorke's Drift and elsewhere; but they preferred to risk their lives to the last, in defence of their weaker comrades, and for the honour of their country. So, they dismounted and let their horses go, and then sold their lives as dearly as possible on that fateful ridge.

Who can tell how the future of the gallant little colony of Natal has been influenced by the heroism of her sons on that memorable occasion?

While we were at Simon's Bay some of us went to Cape Town, where we met Colonel Hassard, the Commanding Royal Engineer. He had been invalided from the front, and he told us a good many stories about what had been going on there. Having heard while at Cape Town that a Remount Committee had been collecting horses for the war, and that we could buy them at a fixed price, we secured a few for our officers, and also to make up the numbers required by the mounted men of my field company. The average price of those we bought was £32.

While we were lying in Simon's Bay, we had two interesting visitors. On my way home from China with the 23rd Company in 1860 we touched at the Cape, and volunteers were called for to stay in that colony instead of continuing the homeward journey. I remember one particularly who elected to stay. He was a nice-looking young Scotchman, named Tennant, and he consulted me in regard to his prospects if he did so. I thought, with the qualifications he possessed, he was just the sort to get on in a rising colony, and I advised him to stay. I must say I did not recognise my old friend the corporal in the well-to-do-looking gentleman who came on board the *Palmyra* at Simon's Bay. But when he reminded me of the circumstances, I recognised him. Asking him what he was doing, he replied that he was Colonial Engineer, with a salary of £600 a year. When I remarked that he was doing very well he said: 'Yes, but not so well as Mr. Jones (the other gentleman who came on board), whom you may remember, Sir, as Sapper Jones. He is now a contractor and one of the richest men at the Cape.'

Needless to say, I was very pleased that these former members of 'the corps' had done so well, and so were all their comrades on board.

I must tell one more story before we go on, and not such a pleasant one. Before arriving at the Cape all the men on board were warned of the peculiar drink that is sold on shore, called 'Cape smoke.' It is a strong stimulant, and the effect even a small quantity has on some men is very great. While our vessel was coaling at Simon's Bay, leave was given, as usual, to a certain number of well-conducted men to go on shore.

Among them was one excellent young fellow, whose name I won't mention; but he did not return with the others. The next morning his body was found close to the landing stage; and from inquiry it was believed that, overcome by the drink of the country, he had walked into the water and been accidentally drowned. We paraded as many of the company as possible to attend his funeral in the naval cemetery at the station, and I took the opportunity to emphasise, by the poor young soldier's example, the necessity of avoiding, with more than usual care, the wine shops of the Cape.

I may add that the lesson had a good effect, for, while regiments could not as a rule be left at Durban on account of the drink there, our men were for over a fortnight in camp at that port without a single crime of any sort being recorded against them.

On April 1, 1879, we left Simon's Bay, and in four days reached Port Natal, or, as it is now called, Durban. The harbour was very shallow, and at that time large vessels had to lie outside the bar, disembarkation being effected by means of lighters. We took a whole day getting on shore with our horses and stores in this way, and then had to struggle along a heavy sandy road, for about two miles, to a standing camp that had been established for the convenience of the troops on first landing.

We soon learned that in South Africa the maxim applied with more than usual force: 'If you want a thing done, do it yourself.' Army requirements were very numerous, and the sappers, the army's workmen, were much appreciated when they landed and got their tools on shore; and soon the whole company were as busy as bees, either getting their own equipment and transport into order, or carrying out the innumerable small services that the Staff of the expedition called upon them to perform.

We heard when we landed at Durban that Brigadier-General Evelyn Wood had repulsed a determined attack by a Zulu '*impi*' on his camp (which was really a fort) at Kambula. In the operations that preceded the attack, Captain Campbell of the Coldstream Guards was killed. In this business the Zulus are said to have lost some 3,000 men, while the British had nine officers and ninety men killed. We heard also that Lord Chelmsford, with a column from Durban, had relieved Colonel Pearson's force at Etshowe, and had beaten off an attacking column of Zulus at a place called Gingilhovo. The British loss was small, but Lieut.-Colonel Northey, of the 60th Rifles, was wounded, and shortly afterwards died.

Major-General Clifford landed on April 7 and took over his new charge, the line of communications. His base was the seaport Durban, where he stayed for a time to start business. Afterwards he went to Pietermaritzburg, the capital of Natal, where he established his headquarters.

It will, I think, be convenient to recount now in general terms Lord Chelmsford's arrangements for the approaching campaign. Having seen personally to the safety of the southern column, he proposed to strengthen it and put it under the command of Major-General Crealock, who had been sent out from England to command a division. This was called the first division. The second division, under the command of Major-General Newdigate, and the cavalry under Major-General Marshall were to proceed up country by regiments, and rendezvous in the vicinity of Dundee. This force was based on Natal, being supplied with ammunition and other special stores by way of Newcastle and Pietermaritzburg.

Brigadier-General Evelyn Wood was to command an independent column, called the flying column, based on Utrecht and the Transvaal, but with another line of communication through Newcastle to the sea at Durban. Colonel Redvers Buller commanded the mounted troops attached to this column. Thus, three independent columns, besides the Cavalry Brigade, were put in position and organised for the advance against the central power of the Zulus at Ulundi.

While at Durban I saw General Clifford, who wished to consult me regarding various engineer matters.

On the 10th I also saw Lord Chelmsford, who had returned after his successful fight with the Zulus at Gingilhovo. He suggested that, if possible, we should bridge the Tugela at its mouth with such pontoons as we had brought out with us from England, supplemented by casks and other material that we could collect locally. This was eventually done by the company. Meantime Captain Blood had completed the equipment of the Field Company with transport suited to the country.

On April 13 I bought a good-looking horse from a man named Lowry for £47. I also bought a gelding from Commissary-General Strickland for £42.

On this day orders were issued for the distribution of the force. Those relating to the Engineers were as follows:

Lieut.-Colonel Steward, Commanding Royal Engineers in the field, will relieve Captain Hime, Colonial Engineer, from his duties as Divisional Officer B.E. in Natal from this date; Brevet Lieut.-Colonel Harrison will accompany and be attached to Headquarters in the field; Captain Blood will be attached to Headquarters of the 1st Division; and Captain Anstey to the 2nd Division; Lieut. Watkins will act as Adjutant under Lieut.-Colonel Steward; Lieut. Cameron will be stationed at the base of operations.'

This very important order, as far as I was concerned, took me away from the command of my Field Company. I did not see it again during the war, for it went to the southern force, *i.e.*, the 1st Division, under General Crealock, while I went with Headquarters, which accompanied the 2nd Division.

On April 15 I was ordered to Pietermaritzburg to await the rest of the Staff there. I utilised this journey to test the marching power of my horses, and to learn a little of the 'art of travelling' in South Africa. On arrival at the capital of Natal, I put up with Captain Hime (R.E.), who at that time was Colonial Engineer and a member of the government of the colony. While with him I fitted myself out for the approaching campaign. It may be asked what I had to do more than had been done already, partly in England before we started, and partly on landing at Durban. Anyone who has had experience of campaigning as a Staff officer, or who knows the difference between travelling with a party conducted by one of Cook's dragomen, and travelling by oneself in a wild country, could answer the question.

I left England and landed in Durban as a regimental officer. My rations were drawn by the quartermaster-sergeant, my cooking was done by the company cooks, my baggage was carried in regimental transport, my tent was pitched and trenches dug by a regimental fatigue party; but when I became a Staff officer, and was liable to march and pitch my camp either by myself or with others, it became necessary to make oneself entirely independent. I knew that the more carefully I organised my establishment before I started, the less would be my trouble afterwards, and the more time I should have to carry out whatever Staff work I might be ordered to do.

So, I refreshed my memory from the heading 'Kit for Staff' in the *Officers' Memorandum Book,* I consulted my host and other officers in Pietermaritzburg on the peculiar requirements of the country, and in a few days, I was ready for a start. At my suggestion a young officer (Lieut. Heneage, A.D.C. to the General of Cavalry) was to go with me and sketch the road for the benefit of those who followed. My cavalcade, as follows, reached Pietermaritzburg on April 22, *viz.* Lance-Corporal Martin, R.E. (a Draughtsman), riding my bat pony; Driver Cook, R.E. (my groom), on my third charger; a Scotch cart, drawn by three horses with one native driver, carrying our baggage and provisions; Driver Burdett, R.E. (my head servant and cook), on my first charger 'Rocket'; and I myself on my second charger, 'Durban.' We carried with us all arrangements for pitching a small camp, and a reserve of food for men and horses. Each mounted man had a saddle-bag, and so we could divide up into two parties at short notice if required.

The first day we reached Howick, a distance of fourteen miles, and there we met the new battalion of the 24th Regiment that had been sent from England to take the place of the one destroyed at Isandlwana, and also some of the Headquarter Staff.

The route we were travelling was through Estcourt, Colenso, and Lady smith. Our immediate destination was Dundee, where the Headquarter Staff was to assemble, and where later on the 2nd Division under General Newdigate, and the Cavalry Brigade under General Marshall, were to concentrate and organise for the advance into Zululand. The road at that time had no special interest, but it was a pretty rough one, and the places along it at which food and forage could be obtained were not regulated with a view to the requirements of an army marching along in detachments.

Then our horses were in bad condition, our drivers were ignorant of the country and of a traveller's requirements, so that we were rather proud of arriving at Dundee on the day that I had calculated before we left Pietermaritzburg, thereby stultifying the prognostications of our knowing friends, who told us that keeping to time was a thing unknown in South Africa.

The day before we reached Ladysmith my second charger ('Durban') got horse-sickness. The day following, he was worse, and, though he was treated with all the usual remedies, he died at night. This was the first occasion on which I met the Prince Imperial of France, who was travelling up country with the General commanding. He took the greatest interest in the illness of my horse, sitting up by him, and helping to apply the remedies ordered by the veterinary surgeon who had charge of the case.

On arriving at Dundee on April 30 I joined the Headquarter Staff. The same day the general held a review of the troops already collected there, *viz*. 21st and 58th Foot, two companies of the 24th, Harness's battery of four guns, and Dartnell's Horse.

Soon after joining I reaped the benefit of the way in which my own personal following had been organised at Pietermaritzburg. For when orders were issued for the force at Dundee, accompanied by the Headquarter Staff, to move to Landman's Drift on the Buffalo River, while the general commanding, with only his military Secretary, two *aides-de-camp* and myself were to go in light order and inspect Wood's force at Kambula, I was ready to fall into the arrangement without any trouble whatever.

On this trip Lord Chelmsford discussed with us the whole position, and made all arrangements for the approaching campaign, as I will proceed to relate. But first let me say a word or two regarding my companions. The general commanding at the Cape, who now had charge of the war against the Zulus, had previously been in command of one of the infantry brigades at

Aldershot, where I had known him.

He was over the average height, good at games and outdoor pursuits, and very fond of his profession, which he had studied carefully when acting as adjutant-general in India, and elsewhere. He was a most reasonable and pleasant chief to deal with, and would always listen to whatever one had to say. I do not think I had a word of disagreement all the time I was with him. Then he was simple and moderate in his habits, and set an example of frugality to all around him.

His military secretary (Lieut.-Colonel North Crealock, 95th Regiment) was a clever Staff officer, particularly skilful with his brush, as was his brother, Major-General H. Crealock, who commanded the 1st Division. His *aides-de-camp* were Captain Molyneux (22nd Regiment), a good saff officer, who was ready to help in any way if wanted; and the young Prince Louis Napoleon, Prince Imperial of France.

The latter, having been educated at the Royal Military Academy, Woolwich, came out as a volunteer to the army in South Africa. He bore a letter from the commander-in-chief to Lord Chelmsford, requesting that assistance should be rendered him to see as much as possible with the columns in the field, and with this view Lord Chelmsford attached him to his personal staff. At this time, he was a particularly smart, nice-looking young officer, with perhaps a touch of sadness on his face. He was very keen to learn all he could of the manner in which we carried on our wars, and of the organisation of our staff and departments, and I had many conversations with him on the subject. He was also anxious to take his part in anything that was going on, and was only too eager for employment in the face of the enemy.

In regard to myself I will only say that for several years I had devoted many hours that might have been otherwise spent to the study of the profession of arms, and just before coming out to the Cape I had passed the final examination at the Staff College.

Starting on May 2, we had a look at the preparations then in progress for the 2nd Division camp at Landman's Drift, passed some men of the 80th Regiment from Wood's Camp cutting firewood on the Doornberg, and a little farther on the 94th Regiment and the 5th Company R.E. (in which was Chard of Rorke's Drift fame). We arrived in the evening at Baltee Spruit, where we found the Headquarters of the 80th in an old Dutch *laager*. The next day we crossed the Blood River and reached Wood's Camp at Kambula, which he had defended not long before against a determined attack by a large Zulu '*impi*.' After a ride to Zunguin Neck, and a look at Inslobani Mountain, where Wood's mounted troops were so severely handled the day before the Kambula attack, we saw an alarm practised at the camp; and on the 6th we went to Utrecht, where Headquarters were to be established until the troops were ready for the advance.

Now, the little party that left Dundee in light order on May 2 had not been idle. Not only had it travelled fast and far, but it had taken part in long animated discussions with all whose opinions were worth having about the conditions of the country, and the best manner of carrying out the approaching war.

There were already in Natal quite sufficient troops to subjugate the Zulus, but there were more than the usual difficulties in regard to transport. The rivers were not navigable; the only railway ran from Durban to Pietermaritzburg; and all movement depended upon sufficient wheel and pack carriage being obtainable to keep the troops supplied with food and ammunition and such other stores as were necessary for the campaign.

Many people think that in a temperate climate you have only to send enough horses and mules with an army to enable it to go anywhere. There was never a greater mistake. Given a seat of war in which no food can be furnished for horses by the country, and it is a simple matter to calculate the distance from the base of supplies that a horse or mule can carry or draw a useful load. It must be borne in mind that under these conditions each animal must bring along his own food as well as whatever else he has to carry; and, even if there are good roads, he will not take a useful load beyond four or five marches—say sixty miles.

In Natal and Zululand, it cannot be said that there was no

food to be obtained for horses. Some mealies are usually grown on white men's farms as well as by Kaffir *kraals*; and at certain times of the year there is plenty of grass. But English horses had to be taught to eat the grass of the country; and mealies, unless carefully administered, often disagree with them. Besides which there was the terrible horse-sickness, not to mention various tormenting flies; so, they could not be considered good transport animals.

Although the fact may be overlooked by those who have only known South Africa since it has been crossed and recrossed by railways, the real transport animal in that country is the bullock. You must treat him properly if you want to get good work out of him. You must not try and make him go too fast; you must give him time to eat the grass that he finds by the roadside, and drink the water of the streams, and also to take periodical rests, and he will be to you on the *veldt* of South Africa what the camel is in the north—the ship of the desert.

The problem before Lord Chelmsford and his Staff, while the columns were concentrating and organising for the advance into Zululand, was how to bring to the various rendezvous the necessary supplies, and where to get the bullock wagons required to move those supplies across the *donga*s of Zululand as far as the capital of that country—the king's *kraals* at Ulundi.

Transport being the ruling factor, only such troops could be taken as could be fed; and the farther the troops marched from the bases of supply, the more difficult it became to feed them. This meant organisation. Which troops were to form the columns of the moving army, and which were to serve on the line of communications? How were the columns themselves to be formed, and what was to be the organisation of the guiding and controlling staff? These questions had, no doubt, been carefully considered by the general commanding ever since he knew what troops were coming out from England to take part in the war. Now was the time to put the finishing touches to the machine, and to set it in motion.

On the morning of May 8 Lord Chelmsford came into my

tent and told me that he had determined to appoint me acting Quartermaster-General of the Army, pending approval from England. Of course, I was much honoured by the confidence thus shown in me, and I said I would do my best; but I was well aware of the difficulties that had to be faced. At that time there was no Quartermaster-General's Department in the country. The work was supposed to be done by the adjutant-general's staff and a new organisation which had charge of the base and the lines of communication, of which General Clifford was the head.

The troops were scattered along a line of communication over 300 miles, which had to be kept up chiefly by runners or special orderlies. No road reports or military sketches of the country existed. There was very little information regarding the enemy, and I had no office whatever, only Lance-Corporal Martin, whom I had brought with me from Pietermaritzburg, and my own private sketching case and stationery.

I knew that three matters were urgent, *viz*. First, the completion of the organisation of the forces; second, the collection of supplies and transport; third, reconnoitring the enemy's country.

That same afternoon an officer, Lieut. Carey, 98th Regiment, was appointed to assist me in military sketching; and the Prince Imperial was lent to me to collect and compile information in regard to the distribution of troops and depots. Having set these two officers to work I drafted and sent off a number of telegrams regarding the collection of supplies.

The next day I was put in orders as assistant-quartermaster-general attached to Headquarters, and it was clearly laid down that I was to be the head of a department, distinct from the adjutant-general, and having authority to send instructions to all officers of the army by means of memoranda.

★★★★★★★★★★

On receipt of Lord Chelmsford's telegram on the subject, the War Office appointed Major East, from the Intelligence Department, Deputy Q.M.G., and gave him the rank of Lieut.-Colonel to enable him to hold the appointment; but he did not arrive until a day or two before the Battle of Ulundi, when the Q.M.G.'s work for the campaign was nearly over.

****

Work began to pour in from all sides, and from that date until I handed over to an officer sent out specially from England I spent the greater part of every day in the saddle, and the greater half of every night writing letters and instructions in my tent. My lamp was the only one allowed to be kept alight after hours.

Of the three urgent matters that required attention when I was appointed A.Q.M.G., the organisation of the forces was taken in hand by Lord Chelmsford himself, in consultation with his Staff, while the collection of supplies and transport and the reconnaissances were left to me. I have said that on the evening of my appointment I sent out to all commanding officers instructions in regard to transport. Looking forward a little, I may say that the transport and supplies for the 1st (Crealock's) Division, operating in the south of Zululand, were furnished by Natal; the transport for the cavalry, concentrating at Dundee, consisted chiefly of Army Service Corps; while that for the 2nd Division (Newdigate's) and Wood's flying column were, to a large extent, hired in the Transvaal.

The latter had the advantage that the owners (Boers) came with their own wagons and bullocks, and naturally took especial care that they were properly looked after. There was no fear of their running away, and, as far as I know, they were thoroughly efficient throughout the whole business. I may add that some months afterwards, when I was commanding in Pretoria, I was able to catch a number of these wagons returning to their farms, and re-engage them for extended service in the war against Sekukuni. Without this timely assistance it would have been difficult, if not impossible, to bring the latter war to a conclusion as rapidly as our new commander-in-chief (Sir Garnet Wolseley) desired.

But to return to the Zulu War. As soon as I was satisfied that everything that could possibly be done had been accomplished to start the collection of transport and supplies for the reorganised forces, I obtained leave from the chief to start the reconnaissances.

The position of the forces at the beginning of May was as follows: Wood's column was still at Kambula; Newdigate's Division was at Landman's Drift; and about half way between the two a fortified post had been established as a base of supply at Conference Hill, on the Blood River. The Cavalry Brigade was at Dundee, and the Headquarters of the army at Utrecht.

The Battle of Ulundi

It was known that the country between the Black and White Umvaloosi Rivers was very difficult, if not impracticable. At the same time, it was known that there were tracks practicable for wagons between Rorke's Drift and the capital. What was required was to ascertain if sufficiently good roads could be made between the rendezvous of the 2nd Division and Wood's column, to enable these forces to join hands and then advance as one army on Ulundi.

The troops available for escort duty were the Cavalry Brigade at Dundee, the mounted troops of Wood's column under Lieut.-Colonel Buller, and Bettington's Natal Horse, at that time at Conference Hill. The Cavalry Brigade were still somewhat unfit for work after their long voyage from England, and they had not yet learned the ways of campaigning in South Africa, while Wood's mounted troops were in good condition, thoroughly acquainted with Zulu customs, and moreover were under the command of an officer who had an eye for country second to none in the army, and who was an exceptionally good leader of mounted men. So, I arranged that for the first reconnaissance I should accompany a mounted party led by Buller. We were to rendezvous at Conference Hill, and a small detachment of Bettington's Horse were also to go with us.

On May 13 the general officer commanding, with his military secretary, left the Headquarter Camp at Utrecht for a trip to Newcastle, and I went off to take part in the reconnaissances in Zululand. I was accompanied by two officers of the Headquarter Staff, *viz.* the Hon. J. Drummond, Chief of the Intelligence Department, and the Prince Imperial, extra *aide-de-camp* to Lord

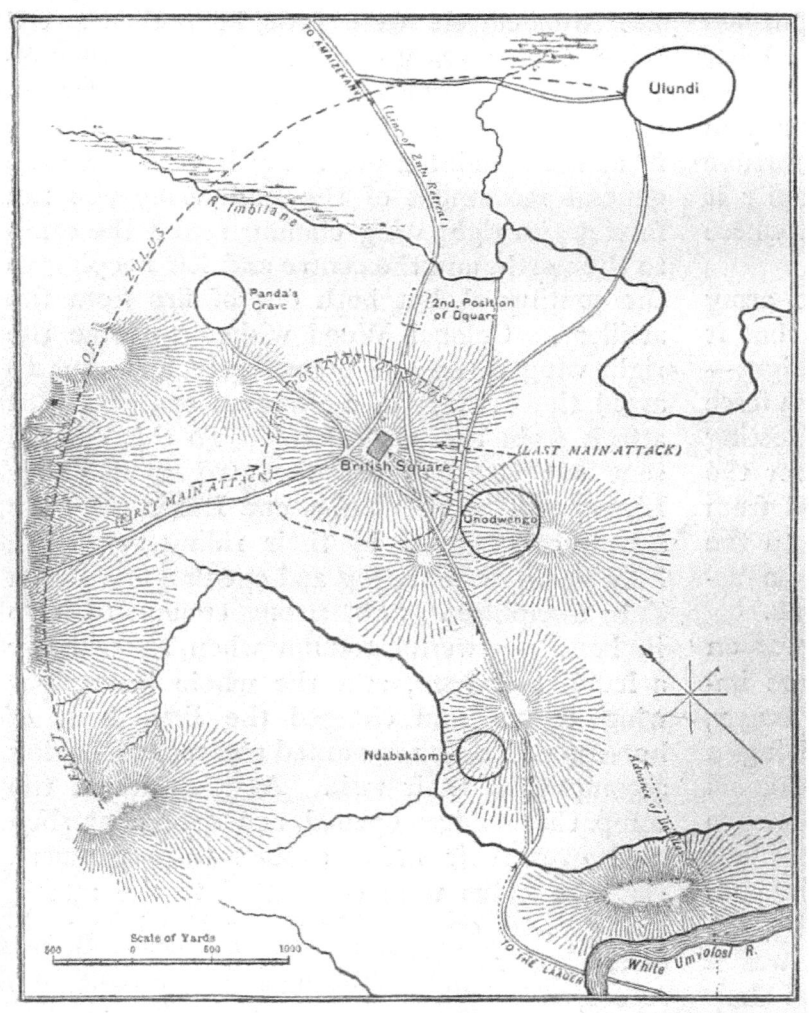

PLAN OF THE BATTLE OF ULUNDI: JULY 4, 1879.

Chelmsford. Each of us took one servant and three horses; all our requirements were carried in saddle-bags.

An easy day's march took us to Conference Hill, where we drew rations for men and horses. The next morning Colonel Buller arrived with some two hundred frontier Light Horse and Basutos, and we went all together to Koppie Allein, where we bivouacked in a deserted farm. The horses were knee-haltered and turned into a mealie field for the night. Fires were lit and food prepared, each one for himself, and then we lay down and slept, in great coats and blankets, on the mud floor of the farmhouse.

At daylight on the 15th, we were off in a southerly direction, Buller leading. At about 10.35 we halted to rest the animals, and boil water to make tea or coffee. All meals on these occasions are much the same—a little tinned meat, some ration bread or biscuit, occasionally as a treat a little potted meat or, perhaps, jam, and then the fragrant and soothing cup of tea or coffee, after which a talk round the smouldering fires, and, if there is time enough, a pipe or cigar.

About the middle of this day, we saw a few Zulu scouts among the hills, some on foot and one or two mounted. We pursued them for some distance and then gave it up, because they did not go in the direction that we wanted to spy out. Once we entered a *kraal* from which the inhabitants had departed, leaving only a few diseased cattle; and then we continued on our way until it was quite dark, when we made a ring of our horses, heads inwards, saddles and bridles on, riders lying down by them on the grass. It was not safe in such a situation to feed by night, because the horses might stray away too far in the darkness; and we could not light fires, because so doing might attract attention. As a rule, the time for rest and food during a reconnaissance is in the daytime, and in a position that can be protected by outposts.

On the 16th we arrived at a new camp that had been established for Wood's column, near Wolf Hill.

Now the three days' march that we had just accomplished, under the guidance and direction of Buller and his mounted

Frontier Light Horse

men, had no doubt been useful to all of us, and it had established certain facts in connection with the Zulus; but it had not discovered a route for the 2nd Division, and so I determined to make a further reconnaissance. This matter I discussed with Colonel Wood when we got in, and we had a long talk regarding plans for the campaign, and then I wrote to Lord Chelmsford and others until far into the night. The next morning Wood went off early to Utrecht to see the commander-in-chief, and I went to Conference Hill, to make arrangements for the further reconnaissance. Drummond went back to Headquarters, but the Prince Imperial, having obtained leave from the commander-in-chief, returned to go with me.

My immediate party for this expedition consisted of the prince and his servant, Captain Carey, D.A.Q.M.G., Captain Bettington with five of his men leading spare ponies, and twenty Basutos under an officer. We had arranged to meet Colonel Buller and some four hundred mounted men at a point eastward of the Ingutu Mountains, but on arrival there we saw nothing of them. The day wore on while we were searching, and we had to spend the night in that vicinity, taking all precautions in case our position and circumstances should become known to any of the Zulus who lived in the neighbourhood.

The next morning, after a further fruitless search for Buller's men, we had to make up our minds what to do: should we return to Conference Hill or get back on to the Ingutu Range, and, proceeding eastward along the ridge, endeavour to find a road leading into the valley of the Nondweni River, and so to Ibabanango Mountain? Captain Bettington told me that he had frequently been in that part of the country with quite a few men, and that safety lay in proper precautions rather than in the size of the escort. So, I agreed to go on. The prince and Captain Carey were both sketching, and Captain Bettington took immediate command, under me, of the mounted men.

Our order of march was as follows: Bettington leading; in front and on the flanks, guided by their leader's hand, Bettington's troopers; close behind, taking notes of the ground as we went along, the Prince Imperial; then myself; and behind me Carey and the Basutos. Our direction was south-east, and our object to find a way up to the top of the Ingutu Ridge.

When ascending a very steep path, up which our horses could hardly scramble, some Zulus lined the rocks at the top and opened fire. The prince dismounted and drew his sword; Bettington pressed on in front, his men firing as they went; and I waved my helmet to urge on the Basutos. Two of the latter galloped up at once, and joined us in the attack, but the rest hung back a little and did not come up until we had won our way to the top. The Zulus began their usual tactics of trying to surround us, but the side of the hill, except on the path, was too steep even for them. Moreover, I think they were surprised by our rapid attack, and did not know what our strength was. Anyhow, they gave way in the centre as we mounted the path, and then the Basutos came up and completed their discomfiture.

At the top we found a large *kraal*, and in it some saddles and other stores taken at Isandlwana. After a short halt there we continued our march. I had started slightly ahead of the escort, when I saw three men in red coats advancing towards me. They were coming along in a leisurely manner, evidently returning to the *kraal* in ignorance of the skirmish that had taken place there, and thinking that it was still occupied by their own people. Their only arms, as far as I could see, were *assegais*.

Not realising at first who they were, whether Natal Kaffirs in British service or followers of Ketchwayo, I approached nearer to them, at the same time changing direction slightly to the right in order to avoid being caught on the path they were using, which ran along the edge of the steep northern slopes of the Ingutu Ridge. At that moment I heard a shout behind me, and saw Bettington, the commander of my escort, coming along the path at a gallop, with his revolver in his hand. Clearly, he did not want any nearer approach to show him who my three friends were, and, riding past me, he shot one of them, while the other two jumped into the bush on the mountain side and disappeared.

When the war was over, I was asked to verify this little incident; and, in connection with other service, it obtained for Captain Bettington the honour of a decoration. Later on, we came upon some horses grazing and captured some of them.

We then went on again along the ridge, descending into the valley of the Nondweni, and reconnoitring up to the slopes of Alarm Hill, near which ran the wagon track from Rorke's Drift to Ulundi. It seemed to me that we had found the road we wanted for the 2nd Division; the 'going' on the top of the Ingutu Hills was good and easily protected, and the only difficulty along the route was the descent to the valley at the eastern end.

Having done what we started to accomplish, we retired. Towards evening we found some wood in a *kraal*, and were able to cook. Then, leaving our fires alight, we went on again. Some Zulus followed us, and when they came to one of our fires they danced round it, making the most hideous noise. So, we did not think it safe to stay long anywhere, but worked our way by stars and compass throughout the night, and early the next morning reached Conference Hill. Even then our troubles were not quite over. We knew that it was the custom of British troops in South Africa, at that time, to turn out before daybreak, and man the defences around the *laager* that they had occupied during the night, as a precaution against possible attacks at dawn of day.

We were aware also that many of the troops were young and inexperienced, and did not always await their officers' orders to fire. So, we approached the *laager* at Conference Hill with caution. It was well we did so. The men were lining the trench that had been dug around the encampment, and we could hear their colonel talking to them: 'Now, boys, be ready—when I give the word to fire, fire low—I see them coming—look out, boys—remember to fire low'; and so on, until, by signals, without showing our bodies, we convinced the gallant defenders of the post that we were not Zulus, but only hungry and tired comrades anxious to obtain food and rest.

The same afternoon the prince and I rode back to Headquarters at Utrecht, leaving our companions at Conference Hill.

Since we left a week ago, we must have ridden over 200 miles. During the last thirty-six hours we were twenty-five in the saddle, but the prince enjoyed it all immensely, and, besides making a very good report, which I forwarded to Lord Chelmsford, he wrote a long account to the Empress of the French in England of all he had seen and done.

At our bivouacs, and elsewhere, we frequently discussed military and other matters, and I had to reply to his many questions about what was the organisation of this and that in the English Army by telling him that the word with us was hardly understood—the usual custom being for our generals to make such arrangements, in the field, as they thought most likely to meet the circumstances of the time. Then he took great interest in hearing from Captain Bettington how he had spent his early life in New Zealand, driving cattle, assisting as a dispenser, keeping a livery stable, and for a time even acting as 'boots' at an hotel, until he found himself in Natal at the time of the Zulu War, and obtained the command of the irregular mounted corps that bore his name.

Arrived at Utrecht, I reported to the general commanding the result of our reconnaissances, soon after which Buller came in, and said that he had gone to what he thought was the rendezvous where I was to meet him, and, not finding us there, had reconnoitred on his own account. His recommendations in regard to the route for the 2nd Division differed from mine, and as he had had considerable experience in the country, and I had had none, the general naturally inclined to his.

At this time the Cavalry Brigade, under General Marshall, made a reconnaissance on a large scale into Zululand; but they did not go much beyond the battlefield of Isandlwana, and their reports threw no light on the best line of advance for the columns. So, it was settled that the 2nd Division was to enter the country by way of Koppie Allein, and to follow generally the route taken by Wood's column, each force being complete in all arms and forming its own *laager* for the night bivouac. Headquarters were to accompany the 2nd Division.

The general line of advance being settled, it became necessary to make detailed reconnaissances, and road sketches, for the convenience of the troops.

To carry out this I had at my disposal Captain Carey, who worked from Conference Hill, and the Prince Imperial, who was to remain at Headquarters, but was to be held available to carry out such quartermaster-general's work as from time to time I might entrust to him. By direction of Lord Chelmsford, I gave the prince written instructions that he was never to leave the immediate precincts of the camp without a proper escort. His ordinary work was to sketch the camps occupied by Headquarters, and the roads they traversed when on the march.

The latter part of May was spent in carrying out the details connected with the organisation of the forces for the combined march, in collecting supplies, and in training the troops of all arms for the anticipated fighting. Wood's column was moving steadily southward, and on May 28 the 2nd Division and Army Headquarters moved to Koppie Allein.

On June 1 the 2nd Division made its first march into Zululand, and the same afternoon one of the most unhappy events in this or any war took place—the death of the gallant young prince, who had come out to share with his comrades of the English Army the risks and dangers of war.

The evening before, he came to me and asked that he might extend his sketch beyond the camp to be occupied the next day, and make a reconnaissance of the road to be traversed the day following. I saw no objection to this, provided he took with him the usual escort. Many of us had been over the ground, and we knew there was no '*impi*' in the neighbourhood. Moreover, I thought that the cavalry which accompanied the division, would be extended over the country far in advance of the camp, so I gave permission. Shortly afterwards Captain Carey came to my tent, and asked that he might go with the prince's party, as he wished to verify his sketch of the country, and I said 'yes,' and added that he could look after the prince, and see that he did not get into any trouble.

On the morning of the 1st, I was told that Carey and the prince were ready to go, but that the escort had not turned up. So, I walked over to see the General of Cavalry, and he sent his brigade-major to make the necessary arrangements. I then took in hand my own work for the day. I rode ahead with the Staff officer of the division, and showed him the site for their camp on the ridge between the Incenci and the Itelezi Hills. I then went to see to the watering arrangements.

While so engaged I came across Carey and the prince, and found that they had with them the European part of their escort, a detachment of Bettington's Horse, but none of the Basutos, whom I had specially ordered to be detailed, because they have a much keener sense of sight and hearing than Europeans, and consequently make better scouts. They told me that they were to get their Basutos from the regiment that was out scouting in front of the camp, and I enjoined them not to go forward without them. Returning to camp, I accompanied Lord Chelmsford round the *laager*, and then went to my tent and drafted the orders for the next day's march.

About six o'clock in the evening Captain Carey came to see me, and reported that the reconnoitring party he was with had off-saddled the other side of the Ityotyozi River, and had been surrounded by Zulus, and that the prince, two of the white men, and the interpreter were missing, as well as five horses. I said: 'You don't mean to say you left the prince?'

And he replied: 'It was no use stopping; he was shot by the first volley.'

And I said: 'You ought to have tried, at all events, to bring away his body.'

Much overcome by what I said to him, he told me, as far as he could remember, the story of what had happened, accepting full responsibility for what had taken place. Immediately afterwards I went to see Lord Chelmsford, and asked him to allow me to go out at once and look for the prince. After what Carey had said I hardly expected to find him alive, but anyhow I thought I might bring home his body. The chief, however, would not let me go;

all he said was, 'I don't want to lose you too.'

Later on, it was settled that the cavalry were to go out at daybreak and search the spot where the fight had taken place; and reports were called for from Carey, Bettington's men, and myself.

The story as it evolved itself was briefly as follows:

When Captain Carey and the prince left me on the Itelezi Hill, they did not, as I had instructed them, look for the Basuto escort, but went on without them. The party consisted of these two officers, six troopers of Bettington's Horse, and a native interpreter (told off by the Chief of the Intelligence Department). The prince did not, as usual, take his servant with him on this occasion, and Captain Bettington did not accompany his men. If either of these had gone, matters might have been different.

(*The next paragraph and the four following ones are taken from the published official account of the war.*)

About half-past twelve they reached a flat-topped hill, on the summit of which they dismounted while the prince made a rough sketch of the surrounding country. After spending an hour on this hill, they moved along the ridge between the Tombokala and Ityotyozi Rivers, and about 2.30 p.m. descended from the high ground towards a *kraal* some 200 yards from the latter stream. This *kraal* was of an ordinary type, and consisted of a circular stone enclosure outside of which there were five huts. The huts were unoccupied, but some dogs were prowling about, and fresh remains of food could be seen, and it was evident that the inhabitants had only recently gone away.

The ground near the *kraal* was covered with coarse grass and Indian corn, growing to a height of five or six feet, and surrounding the huts on all sides except the north and north-east. Here the ground was open for about 200 yards, but at that distance from the *kraal* there was a *donga* or dry watercourse, some six or eight feet deep, by which, in the rainy season, the storm waters found their way into the Ityotyozi.

On arriving at the *kraal*, at about 3 p.m., the prince ordered the escort to off-saddle and knee-halter the horses for grazing. This was done, and the men made coffee and rested until nearly four, when the native guide reported that he had seen a Zulu come over the hill. The horses were at once caught and saddled, and the men prepared to mount.

The prince gave the word to 'mount', and as the word was uttered a volley was fired at the party by a number of Zulus who had crept unobserved through the long grass to within fifteen yards of the huts. Though no one was hit by this volley, the surprise was complete, and the troopers, not yet settled in their saddles, could hardly control their horses, which, terrified by the shots and the yells of the Zulus, bore them across the open ground towards the *donga*.

The prince himself was in the act of mounting when the volley was fired, but his charger becoming restive he appears to have failed to get into the saddle, and to have run alongside the animal, which followed the horses of the escort. The prince, who was extremely active, now endeavoured to vault on to his horse while in rapid motion, but his efforts seem to have been foiled by the tearing of the wallet which he had seized, and on this giving way he fell to the ground, and his horse broke away from him.

As the escort were galloping away from the *kraal* the Zulus kept up a fire by which one trooper was hit in the back and fell. The native guide and another trooper, who had not mounted with the rest, were left behind at the *kraal*, and neither was again seen alive. The remainder of the party, consisting of Captain Carey and four troopers, crossing the *donga* at different points, galloped on for several hundred yards. Captain Carey, after crossing the *donga*, was joined by the rest, and learnt that the prince was not with them, and that he had been last seen between the *kraal* and the *donga*, dismounted and pursued by the Zulus.

Many of the enemy being now on the ground, and the prince's horse being seen galloping riderless at some little distance, Captain Carey came to the conclusion that the prince must have fallen and that it would be useless for the few survivors to return. The party accordingly proceeded in haste to bear the news to the camp of the 2nd Division.

The next morning, early, General Marshall, with a cavalry escort, went to the *kraal* where the reconnoitring party had been surprised. The dead bodies of the two troopers were first found—one in the *donga* and the other between it and the *kraal*; and soon afterwards the body of the prince was found in the *donga*, where he had made his way on foot. Being overtaken there, he had evidently turned on his pursuers, but after emptying his pistol his sword had been of little use against the *assegais* of the enemy, and he had fallen where he stood.

The body, which bore sixteen wounds, all in front, was placed on a bier formed of lances and a blanket, and was carried to an ambulance, on which it was conveyed to the Itelezi Hill Camp. There it was received with all honour, and a service read at a parade of the whole division. Then it was despatched by way of Landman's Drift and Dundee to Pietermaritzburg and Durban, and from thence conveyed in H.M.S. *Orontes* to England, and laid to rest in the mortuary chapel at Chislehurst, from which place it was eventually transferred to Farnborough.

A few words on the events that followed the death of the young prince, and my connection therewith, and then I will return to the march of the columns on Ulundi.

The reports furnished by those who were associated with the Prince Imperial, or who accompanied him on his last fatal ride, led to a court of inquiry, and the court of inquiry led to a court-martial on Captain Carey. While this was in progress war correspondents and others wrote many letters to the papers, and the people in England took much interest in the matter.

It was so sad a thing that a gallant young prince, whose mother lived in England, who had been educated in an English military school, and who had gone out to South Africa to take part in the war that was being carried out there by the land of his adoption, should not only have been killed in a reconnaissance, but have been left behind among the enemy, when some of his comrades galloped off and escaped! Questions innumerable were discussed: Why was he employed on a reconnaissance at all? Why was not the escort larger? Why was it not composed of regular cavalry? What was Captain Carey's business in the matter? &c., &c., and, without waiting for the report of the court of inquiry, or the court-martial, many drew their own conclusions and added to the correspondence.

Among soldiers in South Africa the whole blame for the disaster rested on Captain Carey. In England, at first, it was the same; but when Carey's friends joined in the correspondence, some of the Press took up the line that he was being made a scapegoat of, and, in order to foster this idea, it was necessary to suggest that there were others who were not blameless. I was attacked because there had been a mistake in regard to the escort, and because the duties of the prince when he went out were not defined with greater clearness. Naturally I saw nothing of these Press criticisms until long afterwards, and, even then, I did not think it my duty to answer them; and so, blame rested on me until I returned to England.

I have already said that the court of inquiry led to a court-martial to try Captain Carey. The charge preferred against him by the adjutant-general in South Africa was to the effect that he had shown cowardice in the face of the enemy when in command of an escort.

Naturally Carey did all he could to refute the charge, directing his attention particularly to that part of it which combined the alleged act of cowardice with the fact that he was in command of the party. He was assisted in his defence by an able officer detailed for the purpose, and no one connected with the court-martial thought it necessary to take exception to the statements made in his defence, even though, in trying to save himself, he threw blame on others.

When the court-martial had completed their work, the proceedings were sent to the Horse Guards for the decision of the commander-in-chief. On August 16 an official letter was written to the General commanding in South Africa, stating that the charge against Captain Carey was not sustained by the evidence, and that he was to be released from arrest, and sent to do duty with his regiment.

This letter was sent to me when I was commanding the troops in the Transvaal, and as it contained some observations on my conduct, evidently based on statements made by Captain Carey and others at the court-martial, I replied in full, giving my own version of the occurrence.

The answer to my protest was to the effect that the matter should now be allowed to rest. So, I tried to forget the circumstance, and turned with all the zeal in my power to the work that I had to do in the Transvaal. When that work was over, I was offered a renewal of my appointment by the High Commissioner. At the same time, he said that, as he anticipated that I should only have ordinary routine peace work to carry out, and no opportunity for active service, he would advise me not to take it, but to go home. I acted on his advice and returned to England. Not long afterwards I was given one of the best appointments open to a young officer in England—that of Assistant Quartermaster-General at Aldershot.

I will now return to the campaign in Zululand.

We left Newdigate's Division on June 2 encamped between the Incenci and Itelezi Hills. Wood's column on the same day reached a position near the junction of the Tombokala and Ityotyozi Rivers. Henceforward the movements of the two forces were regulated by orders from Headquarters.

It was anticipated that an attack might be made by the Zulus on the marching columns by day, or against the encampments by night; and so, all the troops were drilled to take up defensive positions round the baggage wagons by day, or to man the *laagers* by night.

The system of the advance was as follows: First thing in the morning the cavalry of each column left the camp of the previous night, and, passing through the infantry outposts, spread out over the country so as to protect the other troops. As soon as a report was received from the commanding officer of cavalry that all was safe, the infantry outposts were withdrawn. The marching columns were then formed, and the march began. Later on Staff officers were sent forward to select the bivouacs for that evening, and, when the troops arrived there, the wagons were formed into a *laager*, trenches were made, if thought necessary, the troops encamped round the wagons, outposts were thrown out, and animals were sent to feed and water. The cavalry then came in.

In case of alarm at night the troops pulled down their tent poles and ran to their stations in the trench around the wagons, or, in case there was no trench, to those on the wagons themselves.

Naturally it took time to teach the men how to make these arrangements quickly and easily, especially as many of those in the ranks were exceptionally young and inexperienced. But careful training and constant practice for the first few days worked wonders.

While, however, the men and officers were learning their duties, the progress made towards Ulundi was far from satisfactory. The route taken was found more difficult than was expected. The '*impedimenta*' of the columns were greater than necessary. The English horses had not yet learned to feed on the grass, and their officers demanded for them full rations; fuel had to be supplied to the troops for cooking purposes; and, finally, a reconnaissance in force, undertaken by the General of Cavalry, showed that the regular trooper fresh from England was of no use against the Zulus in rough and bushy country.

Three days' experience of the organisation under which we had commenced the campaign convinced Lord Chelmsford of the truth of what I had been putting forward to him by word of mouth and in writing for some time past, *viz*. that unless we reduced very materially the size of our marching columns, and established posts on the line of communications, we should never get to Ulundi.

On June 5th, having found some wood on the Zunguin Range sufficiently good for cooking-purposes, a change in the plan for the advance was approved by the commander-in-chief. The 2nd Division were to cut and pile wood, while a portion of the flying column, with all spare wagons, was to go back to

Landman's Drift and Conference Hill, and bring to the front as much food as they could carry.

At the same time orders were issued about horses grazing, and the horse ration was diminished. Moreover, posts were established at certain points, and provided with garrisons, which included a portion of mounted men to enable them to scout the neighbouring country, and render the transmission of convoys possible.

By these means the forces were able to start again on the 17th inst., and to march without any further delay to Ulundi.

From the time when the advance began a permanent escort had been detailed for me, so that I could go from column to column, or visit the cavalry outposts, and thus keep the commander-in-chief acquainted with all that was going on.

The columns starting from the vicinity of the Upoko River on June 18th, 1879, were: Brigadier-General Wood's, comprising three battalions of British infantry, two batteries of artillery, one company of Engineers, and some Irregular Horse under Colonel Buller; and Major-General Newdigate's, with four battalions of infantry, two batteries of artillery, one company of Engineers, besides two squadrons of the 17th Lancers, and a few Irregular Horse under Colonel Drury Lowe.

Wood's column led, as it had done from the commencement; but orders for the operations were issued from Headquarters, which accompanied Newdigate's force. Some instructions were issued for the posts on the line of communications, and also for Major-General Marshall, who, with the larger part of the Cavalry Brigade, was put in charge of the general defence of the country, and the line of communications of the advancing columns.

On the 18th I accompanied Buller on a reconnaissance to within a mile or two of the Umlatoosi River. We saw a few Zulu scouts on the hills, burning grass.

Comparatively speaking, short marches were made by both columns on the 18th, 19th, and 20th. The inexperience of the troops, officers and men, to which I have already alluded, was very evident, especially in the 2nd Division. I find a remark in my journal to the effect that 'I used to take far more pains about the march-out of the pontoon troop that I commanded at Aldershot than is shown here by the Staff in arranging for the march of a division in an unknown country, with such an active enemy as the Zulu in our front. The whole army requires instruction in the art of war.'

But Lord Chelmsford was indefatigable in his endeavours to put things straight, and established some system in the business.

On June 21 I made the usual arrangements for the marches, and selected a site for the new fort on the line of communications. In the afternoon I took a few Royal Engineers out to blow up rocks on the road. The next day I rode out reconnoitring with some of Buller's cavalry, and we had a good view of Ulundi. The quartermaster-general's work was nearly complete—that is to say, the troops had been brought safe and sound to within sight of the enemy, and it only remained to issue the orders for the battle, which, as a rule, is the business of the adjutant-general's branch.

At this juncture Major East arrived at our camp, and took charge of the quartermaster-general's duties. At the special request of Lord Chelmsford, I remained as his assistant; but it was not the same thing. Whenever I reconnoitred, I could not go straight to the general commanding, as I had done hitherto, and tell him what I had seen, and settle at once any required action. I had to report through my new chief. Moreover, not being the head of a department, I no longer attended at Staff conferences, and consequently did not always know what was going on. Nearly the last thing I did, while I was still in charge, was to send a special messenger to General Crealock, who commanded the 1st Division in the south of Zululand, directing him what action to take in concert with the northern columns.

As assistant quartermaster-general I continued to carry out the daily reconnaissances in front of the columns, usually in company with Buller, who commanded the mounted troops of the leading column. East came part of the way with us on June

24, along what was known as the Jackal Ridge. The next two days there were some skirmishes with the Zulus, and one or two military *kraals* were burned.

On the 27th both columns reached the end of the Entonjaneni Range, from whence we looked down over the bush country to the valley of the White Umvolosi River, on the left bank of which lies Ulundi.

Here we made a fortified *laager*, and left all weak men as well as a large number of wagons and oxen, and about one hundred effective horsemen; and, with the balance of the force, lightly equipped, without tents, but with ten days' food, and a good reserve of ammunition, we marched down from the high ground to come to close quarters with the Zulu king. Some oxen and tusks had been sent out from Ulundi as a peace offering, to try and detain us; but Lord Chelmsford would not stop unless all the conditions laid down when we crossed the frontier were fulfilled to the letter.

While we were forming the *laager*, alarming but quite unnecessary reports were circulated about an '*impi*' being near at hand. Those of us who had been constantly with the mounted troops in touch with the Zulus, and had learned something of their manners and customs, knew better. The alarms were started by officers provided with telescopes, who mistook the meaning of the drills and 'doctoring' going on in Ulundi.

On June 20 the two columns, each with one hundred wagons, left the Entonjaneni camp at 9 a.m. More reports were received of possible '*impi*' attacks, and the oxen were hurried along as quickly as possible, and *laager* formed by 1 p.m. More messengers came from the Zulu king, bringing the Prince Imperial's sword, but our chief would no longer delay the advance. At this time, it was quite warm in the plain, compared to what we had experienced on the hillsides during our advance.

On July 1 we started again at 7 a.m., Wood's column, as usual, in front. I went ahead to choose camping-ground, or ground to fight on, if fighting became necessary. I arrived at a *koppie* near the drift across the Umvolosi at 10.40, and from there watched the Zulu Army manoeuvring in and around Ulundi.

Every now and then it looked as if they were coming against us, especially about 11.40; but those who knew their habits felt pretty sure that these demonstrations did not mean an attack, so I proceeded to choose the camping-ground for the two columns close together, about three-quarters of a mile from the drift, and directed the Staff officers on them. But before the flying column had completed its *laager*, and while the 2nd Division wagons were on the road, an order came to me from Lord Chelmsford to complete the *laagers* in half an hour, 'as the Zulus were advancing rapidly towards us, and were then only three miles off.'

I knew that both the *laagers* could not be formed at the place I had chosen under two to three hours, and so I ordered the 2nd Division wagons to park on a hill which I remembered about a mile back. This was done, and the troops formed round them, and set to work with a will to dig the usual defence trenches, so that by the time given both columns were ready for the attack. The Zulus, however, halted near us and did not come on. The *laagers* were then finished with more or less regularity.

That evening we received messages from Sir Garnet Wolseley that he had arrived in Natal, and was going to join General Crealock's column, and from Crealock that he was 'burning *kraals*.'

About 12 o'clock at night there was a scare in both *laagers*. One of the sentries on outpost duty over the 2nd Division fired at an officer who had not answered his challenge, and this so alarmed the native troops that they rushed helter-skelter into the *laager*. I shall not easily forget the occurrence. I was lying down with my great coat on, under one of the wagons, my head sheltered in my saddle, as was the usual custom in South Africa, when I was awakened from my first sleep by the noise of the rush, and saw a naked Zulu dripping with blood, his *assegai* in his hand, standing over me.

In my waking moments the truth flashed upon me, that my visitor was one of the Natal Zulus fighting on our side, who had been frightened by the outpost fire, and had dashed through the

THE ZULU WAR: THE BATTLE OF ULUNDI; INSIDE THE SQUARE.

thorny abattis, which accounted for his appearance. But others did not come so quickly to the same conclusion, and there was a considerable stampede, that it took some time to settle. Among others, the officer who was bivouacking next to me disappeared with my sword, and I did not find it until the next day. Directly I got up I went to where I knew Lord Chelmsford was lying, and I found him just starting round the *laager*, and so I accompanied him. We were pleased to find the regulars all at their alarm-posts and everything ready for a real attack if one had taken place.

The next day the *laagers* were rearranged, and a small stone fort commenced. It was the intention again to divide the force, leaving in the fort and *laagers* all transport and all troops not actually required, and to march against Ulundi with only effective rifles and the pick of our mounted men. A few shots were fired by the Zulus at our men bathing in the river, but, notwithstanding this attention, I could not refrain from going to have a dip too.

On July 3, Buller, with all his mounted men, made an armed reconnaissance, with a view to choosing a good position for the morrow's battle.

There was a great row that afternoon, and nearly all that night, among the Zulu *kraals*. We heard that it was caused by the arrival of Dabulamanzi and his army, who had come from his position in front of Crealock's Division to help his royal brother.

The orders for the battle detailed the troops to defend the *laager* under Colonel Bellairs, the adjutant-general, and also those to advance against the *kraals*. The latter numbered some 3,000 rifles and 900 cavalry.

At about 6.30 a.m. on July 4 our advanced guard of mounted infantry crossed the drift over the river. Meanwhile the cavalry under Buller had crossed lower down, and turned the hill that fronted our advance. Our column, which was composed partly of the flying column, and partly of the 2nd Division, was so organised that it could at any moment be formed into a hollow square, the sides being British infantry, guns at the angles, and inside all the native troops, and mounted officers, and hospitals, &c. There was room also for the cavalry inside the square, and they came there as soon as they had finished their first work of drawing on the enemy.

At about 8 a.m. the combined column arrived at the first ridge, and we saw the Zulus collecting, *viz.* about six companies to the west and twelve companies to the north, some 1,500 yards off; also a large number to eastward near Ulundi.

We passed the Nondwengo *kraal*, and arrived on the ridge, (curiously enough this was also the position which the Zulu king had chosen for his attack on us), chosen the day before by Colonel Buller as the site for the battle, and here we at once formed our square.

The Zulus seemed to spring out of the ground and advanced against us from all sides. They were at first met by the cavalry, which, retiring before superior numbers, took refuge, as arranged, inside the square. The fight began at nine. In twenty minutes to half an hour the fire was pretty hot; a mounted officer on my left had his horse wounded; the animal was in great agony, and the rider, who could not steady his hand sufficiently to shoot his favourite, asked me to perform the merciful act of putting the horse out of its misery. So, I dismounted and did as he requested. At 9.30, the Zulus appearing to waver, the men cheered; at 9.40 they began to retire, and the cavalry were let out of the square to attack them.

Prisoners told us that the whole Zulu Army were present, numbering some 25,000 men, and that the king watched the fight from a hill.

After the battle I rode up to the king's *kraal*, which, like the others, was simply a large barrack, with an apartment at the end; I got from there two wooden milk jugs and some *assegais* and shields. At about two, after the wounded had been attended to, the force started to return to camp. My horse had been grazed by a bullet, and my servant Burdett's gaiter was grazed too.

Among the killed was the Hon. J. Drummond, chief intelligence officer; and the same evening his Zulu scout, by name 'Melinder,' came and attached himself to me, and would not leave me until the war was completely over and I started for

England.

By the action of Ulundi, the Zulu military power was completely broken, and a conviction was brought home to the fighting men whom Ketchwayo had assembled there that their superiority in numbers was of no avail against the weapons and discipline of British troops, even on the open ground where there were no entrenchments.

The news of Lord Chelmsford's victory reached Sir Garnet Wolseley on his way to Port Durnford, where he had intended to join the 1st (Crealock's) Division. This led to various changes in the disposal of the troops throughout the seat of war, but, pending the receipt of fresh instructions, Lord Chelmsford acted on those previously received; thus, the Flying Column was ordered to march to Kwamagwasa, and the 2nd Division to return to Koppie Allein. The staff accompanied the Flying Column, and we arrived at our destination on July 11, having suffered a good deal from wet and cold while marching along the high ground.

At Kwamagwasa, which was an old mission station, we commenced the construction of a fortified post, and then we continued our march to another mission station called St. Paul's, from whence there was a lovely view over the thorn bushes that abound in the valley of the Umlatoosi as far as the mouth of the river and the sea. Here we met Sir Garnet Wolseley and his Staff. On the 16th he inspected the Flying Column, which had been brought to a very efficient condition under the command of Colonel Evelyn Wood.

That evening Sir Garnet told me that he had appointed me to the command of the Flying Column in place of Wood, who was going to England on sick certificate.

The next day our new chief, who was also High Commissioner, went off to a conference of Zulu chiefs at Amangwene *kraal*, while Lord Chelmsford with his personal Staff rode off by way of Ekowe to Durban, to go home by the next mail. (His personal Staff consisted Lieut.-Colonel J. N. Crealock, 95th Regiment; Captain Molyneux, 22nd Regiment; Lieut. Frere, Rifle Brigade; Lieut. Milne, R.N.; Captain E. Buller, Rifle Brigade; Surgeon-Major Scott). I rode with them to say goodbye, and was very sorry to part with my old chief, who was as kind and nice as ever.

It rained more or less all day and continued raining hard all night. On return I shifted my things to the Headquarter camp of the Flying Column, and took over my new command.

On July 18, E. Wood, Buller, and Moysey went away, accompanied by Basutos, who were going back to their homes in Basutoland. As I had done the day before, I rode part of the way with these three officers with whom I had been so closely connected throughout the campaign. On leaving them Buller was kind enough to express his satisfaction at the way in which we had worked together, saying: 'I shall be glad to serve under you again.'

To which I replied: 'It will be the other way next time.'

My Staff with the column consisted of Major Clery, Captain Woodgate, and Captain Prior. The latter was my orderly officer.

****

Major J. E. H. Prior was a brave and capable officer. When with his regiment (the 80th) at Luneberg he heard that some mounted Zulus were in the vicinity of the camp. Attended only by his soldier servant he went out on horseback to find them, and pursuing them for some miles, came up with them and commenced a rifle duel, his servant holding his horse while he dismounted and fired. The Zulus returned the fire. Eventually he killed two, and the rest got away. The next day it was discovered that those he had shot were men of note, one being the celebrated chief, Umbelini. After this adventure Prior became orderly officer to Colonel Redvers Buller, who commanded the mounted troops of Wood's column, and he was mentioned in despatches for gallant conduct.

On leaving me he rejoined the 80th and eventually commanded the 2nd battalion of that regiment. He was a good steeplechase rider.

****

My command was not of long duration; for when Sir Garnet had sent home all the generals except Clifford, he divided the forces as follows: Two columns, one under Lieut.-Colonel

Baker Russell, and one under Lieut.-Colonel M. Clarke, to occupy Zululand and capture the King Ketchwayo; a force under me to hold the Transvaal and reconnoitre Sekukuni's stronghold; and the rest under Major-General the Hon. A. H. Clifford, with headquarters at Pietermaritzburg.

Previously to taking up my new command I was to assist in the organisation of the columns in Zululand, and establish certain posts on the lines of communication. In carrying out these duties I was again impressed by the want of war training in our army. In many cases the marches were without order, the camps without protection.

On August 2, accompanied by Captain Prior and with a small party of servants and transport, I left St. Paul's. My destination was the new Headquarter camp, which was to be established near Ulundi, and where I was to meet Sir Garnet Wolseley and his Chief of the Staff (Colley), to report what I had done so far, and receive fresh instructions. As soon as we had organised our camp and marching arrangements, we got along very well and comfortably, and we made good marches. Nothing of special interest occurred on the road, and we reached our destination on August 7.

The next day I had interviews with the staff and received definite orders to go to the Transvaal. My instructions were to proceed in the first place to Lydenburg, Fort Weeber, and the posts in the vicinity of Sekukuni's country; and then to take over the command of the troops in the Transvaal, with headquarters at Pretoria. Sir Garnet favoured me with his personal views of the situation, and his Intelligence Officer (Maurice) gave me all the information he was in possession of. The Chief of the Staff (Colley) then gave me my orders, and on August 10 I set off on my new errand.

The Transvaal in 1879

The Zulu War was practically over—Lord Chelmsford, Evelyn Wood, Buller, and other officers who had not been so much before the public as those named, had gone to England to be made much of—and Sir Garnet Wolseley, the new commander-in-chief, had redistributed the troops in South Africa as follows: a column, under Lieut.-Colonel Baker Russell, was to operate in Northern Zululand with orders to capture Ketchwayo, the fugitive King of the Zulus, and pacify the country; another column, under Lieut.-Colonel Mansfield Clarke, was to operate in Southern Zululand; while I was to proceed to Sekukuni's stronghold, with orders to reconnoitre there and report on the position, and then take command of the troops in the Transvaal. Besides these, Major-General the Hon. H. Clifford was to take charge of all communications and command the troops in Natal.

On August 10, 1879, at the Headquarter Camp near Ulundi, where the decisive battle against the Zulus had lately been fought, I received my final instructions contained in a memorandum from Sir George Colley, the Chief of the Staff, and a *vivâ-voce* communication from Sir Garnet Wolseley. The former gave me all instructions regarding my approaching journey, while the latter explained what was known of the situation of affairs in the Transvaal and expressed the wishes of the commander-in-chief. As was natural, on the receipt of these orders I did my utmost to make myself acquainted not only with the present circumstances of the country to which I was going, but also what was the feeling of the inhabitants in regard to English rule.

Having previously (though only for a short time) succeeded Colonel Evelyn Wood in the command of the Flying Column, I had had the opportunity of talking to some of the Boers who belonged to that force, and from them I gained a good deal of information. I knew that the South African Boers were the descendants of the early Dutch settlers who had held the whole of the Cape Colonies until their territory was conquered by the English, and formally ceded to Great Britain by the treaty of Paris in 1815. I knew that the domination of the English had always been more or less unwelcome to the Dutch inhabitants, and that about 1834 the antagonism grew into a strong feeling of disaffection towards the English Government.

The story of the Boers in South Africa, told very briefly, is as follows:—

From the year 1830 to 1840 large parties of them, in their endeavour to get away from English rule, crossed the Orange River, the northern frontier of the Cape Colony, and established an independent community, which they called the Orange River Republic. In 1845, soon after the settlement of Natal as an English colony, an Act of Parliament was passed in England providing that the English courts at the Cape should have jurisdiction beyond the Orange River; and Sir Harry Smith, the Governor, issued a proclamation constituting the territory beyond the Orange River a British dependency.

On this the Boers, who had established the settlement between the Orange and the Vaal Rivers, aided by those who had gone north of the Vaal, took up arms, under the leadership of Andries Pretorius, the conqueror of the Zulu King Dingaan.

But after a short campaign they were beaten by the British troops under Sir Harry Smith, in a pitched battle at Boom Plâats. Notwithstanding this victory, however, it was arranged that the British supremacy should not extend further north than the Vaal River, the Boers being permitted to establish an independent State there called the Transvaal Republic. This arrangement was ultimately confirmed by a formal treaty concluded in 1852, and the Dutch emigrants then proceeded to elect a President and constitute themselves into a State.

It seems worth mentioning that, in forming their constitution, they included in it an important declaration which they called the 'Fundamental Law,' to the effect that they did not admit equality of persons of colour with white inhabitants, either in State or Church.

This was in direct contradiction to the English custom, which had been accepted in Natal, that there should be no distinction of language, colour, origin, or creed under the British Flag. In 1854 the English Government, after some discussion in Parliament, arrived at the conclusion that it would be as well to let the Boers do what they liked, not only across the Vaal, but also over the Orange River. Moreover, they handed over to the young Republic there three guns, and all the public offices and furniture. Upon this the Dutch re-established the 'Orange Free State' with a constitution altogether separate from that of the Transvaal; and, being fortunate in its government, this little State soon became compact and prosperous.

It was not the same, however, with its sister State, 'The Transvaal Republic,' which from the first got into trouble with the natives occupying the border territory. In the year 1877 disagreements regarding land boundaries arose between the Boers of the Transvaal and the Zulus; and this brought the Republic into collision with Sekukuni, a powerful ally of Ketchwayo, who lived with a large following in a natural fortress near the Lydenburg Settlements, and who was persuaded by the Zulu king to take sides with him against the white colonists.

When the Boers advanced against Sekukuni's stronghold they were signally defeated; and when, added to this defeat, they seemed also to be on the point of being over-run by the Zulus from the South, the English Government as a matter of defence took possession of the country. The ostensible reason given for this step was that a strong majority of inhabitants of the Transvaal desired annexation by the English. To this reason might be added the hope that, by the action thus taken, a widely spread conflict between the white and black races in South Africa would be prevented.

But whatever the reason given or imagined, the fact remains that there was at the time no opposition. The annexation was carried out by Sir Theophilus Shepstone, the English Commissioner, with a force consisting of twenty-five police. In one particular, however, this somewhat hasty act was attended by a result that was not anticipated. It proved to be more distasteful to Ketchwayo than to the Boers, and probably was the cause of the Zulu War.

The Zulu War I have dealt with earlier. It attracted a good deal of attention in England because of the disaster that attended our arms at the first commencement of hostilities, when a Zulu *'impi'* broke in upon and completely annihilated the British camp at the advanced base of the principal attacking force. This interest was kept up by the departure to the seat of war of large reinforcements, including much extra staff and many war correspondents. But no sooner did the war show signs of coming to a conclusion, than the bulk of the Staff and special correspondents returned home, and the people of England busied their heads no more with the affairs of South Africa.

The result of this was that little, if anything, has been published describing the events that followed the Zulu War, and what little was written has been forgotten. Even in an important publication like the *Encyclopaedia Britannica* the article on the Transvaal is a very meagre one. The only account given of that period is that, in the beginning of 1879, Shepstone was recalled, and Colonel Owen Lanyon, an entire stranger to the Boers and their language, was appointed administrator; that in April of the same year Sir Bartle Frere visited Pretoria, and assured the Boers that they might look forward to complete self-government under the Crown of Great Britain; but that they continued to agitate for independence, and, with the exception of Piet Uys and a small band of followers who served under Colonel Evelyn Wood, they held entirely aloof from our conflict with the Zulus.

The only other allusion in that book to the affairs in the Transvaal in 1879 is that when Sir Garnet Wolseley, who succeeded Sir Bartle Frere as High Commissioner for Natal and the Transvaal, had settled the Zulu question, he proceeded to Pretoria and organised an expedition against Sekukuni, and that Sekukuni's stronghold was captured and his forces disbanded.

It is this little-known page in history that I am now dealing with.

Sir Garnet Wolseley's feelings at the time when he gave me the command in the Transvaal can be gathered from the despatch he wrote to the Secretary of State for War at the end of June, when he first arrived in Natal, which was before the Zulus had been beaten at Ulundi. The following is an extract from it:—

Colonel Lanyon, C.B., C.M.G., Administrator of the

Government of the Transvaal, having informed me that he proposes undertaking operations against Sekukuni at once, I have ordered him not to undertake these operations, to confine himself strictly to defensive measures, and not to raise any more Colonial forces than such as may be absolutely necessary for police and border defence. Not only is the expenditure in the Transvaal apparently growing beyond bounds, but I consider that it would be most unwise to attempt operations against Sekukuni unless with a force sufficient to ensure a certainty of success. Colonel Lanyon has not such a force, and the result of another check from Sekukuni, who can already boast of his successes over the Boers, and the failure of Colonel Rowland's operations against him, might be disastrous, and tend to raise other tribes against us. When Ketchwayo is defeated, I hope to be able to arrange matters with Sekukuni amicably, without sending a military expedition against him. If I fail to do so I shall at least have amply sufficient troops at my command to deal with him by force of arms.

On August 10, 1879, I started from Army Headquarters for the Transvaal. My retinue consisted of Captain Prior, 80th Regiment, who had been appointed my orderly officer, four soldier servants, Captain Prior's native servant, called 'Jack,' a Zulu chief, by name 'Malinder' (who had attached himself to me ever since the Battle of Ulundi), four mule drivers and leaders, six horses and twelve mules, with two Scotch carts. This little party was carefully 'told off' and trained to carry out all the duties of the march and the camp; and, as soon as the animals were in condition, it could do a very fair distance in a day.

Its route, at first, was back along the road traversed by Lord Chelmsford's columns from Utrecht to Ulundi; it reached Fort Evelyn (a distance of twenty-eight miles) the evening of the day it started; the next day it passed Ibabanango Spruit and Fort Marshall, and reached Fort Newdigate (thirty-two miles); on the 3rd day, after halting near the Tombokola River, it arrived at

Conference Hill on the Blood River (thirty miles); and the 4th day it reached Utrecht (twenty-four miles).

During the halt at the Tombokola River I picked some fern and a piece of white stone from the spot on the *donga* where the prince imperial lay when he was killed by the Zulus; these I sent to Sir Lintorn Simmons for the Empress of the French. At Conference Hill I found Colonel Alexander and the Headquarters of the King's Dragoon Guards. The squadrons were out in various directions doing useful work under their majors—one of them, under Major Marter, not long afterwards captured the Zulu King Ketchwayo, in the forest eastward of the Umvoloosi River.

At Utrecht a halt was made to obtain information, and arrange for further progress. I knew this station well, for it was here that Lord Chelmsford's Headquarters were established while the columns were being organised for the final advance into Zululand. From the first I had wondered why the Boers did not afford more direct help to the British in carrying on the Zulu War. It must have been greatly to their advantage that the powerful savage army, organised by Ketchwayo, which had always been more or less hostile to them, and had disputed their possession of land along the Buffalo River, should be suppressed. Certainly a few Boers, old and young, were attached to Wood's column; and their leader, Piet Uys, who was killed on the Slobani Mountains, was one in a thousand. Moreover, a good deal of bullock transport, driven by Boers, was with the British Army in the field; but this latter was well paid for.

When halting again at Utrecht, on the outskirts of what had been a great Boer Republic, but was now, for a time at all events, a portion of the British Empire, I could not help thinking of the problems that faced all administrators in South Africa, and wondering whether in my new command I should be able to solve any of them. In regard to the Boers, I wanted to know if it was their wish that Sekukuni, who had been such a thorn in their side hitherto, should be beaten by the English, as Ketchwayo had been. What would they do to help in this matter? Were the majority of them content that the future of their country should be worked out under the British Flag?

Lastly, what description of self-government would satisfy them? Truly much 'intelligence' work would have to be set in motion to find out, even approximately, what were the opinions held by those in authority among the Boers, and what consequent action would be likely to take place. Many careful arrangements, too, would have to be made to carry out the orders received from the commander-in-chief at Ulundi.

My instructions from the chief of the staff were to go *via* Wesselstroom, direct to Lydenburg. But, finding that the post-cart had been taken off that route, and that consequently there would be no chance of getting supplies of food or animals on that road, I determined to go myself, by the ordinary post-cart, *via* Pretoria, to Sekukuni's country, and to leave my orderly officer to bring the men and horses by ordinary marches to Pretoria, to wait for me there.

Before railways existed in South Africa there were only two ways of getting about the country, *i.e.*, by bullock waggon or by post-cart. The first was slow but 'self-supporting': that is to say, the transport animals (the bullocks) were able to live on the grass of the country if they were given due time to feed and rest. The second was quicker, but it entailed using a road along which supplies for men and animals were procurable. If time was no object, and you wanted to take all your goods and chattels with you, you went by bullock waggon, and your comfort depended a great deal on the size of your retinue.

But if you wanted to get from one place to another as quickly as possible, you either went in a government post-cart or chartered carts and horses of your own, using the depots of supplies that always existed on the post-cart routes.

On August 14 I started from Utrecht in a commissariat two-wheeled cart, with only a pair of saddle-bags, for Newcastle. There I put up at the Masonic Hotel, and at once began collecting information from the innkeeper, who knew Sekukuni's country, and had served in the Boer war against that chief.

In travelling by post-cart in South Africa in those days there was always a good deal of discomfort, and often a certain amount of adventure. Later on, in passing through the Orange Free State, I found myself on one occasion requisitioned by the High Sheriff to help him in securing a notorious horse-stealer, whom he had caught on the *veldt* after an exciting and somewhat dangerous chase. We three (the prisoner in irons) rode together many miles balanced on the post-bags, discussing the advantages and disadvantages of straight shooting in relation to the capture that had just been made.

Another time, in a more crowded cart, but still a two-wheeled one, in galloping recklessly down the slopes of the Drakenberg, I observed that the linchpin had dropped out of one of the wheels, and I was just able to make the driver pull up, to find that by only one-sixteenth of an inch was the cart saved from a smash over a precipice hundreds of feet deep. But in the journey from Newcastle to Pretoria nothing particular happened, and I reached the capital of the Transvaal on the afternoon of the 18th. At that time the administrator and his staff were away from headquarters, so I arranged with the commissariat to lay on special carts; and I started again on the 20th, doing over fifty miles the first day, and reaching Lydenburg (181 miles) on the afternoon of the 24th.

In the journey from Utrecht to Pretoria I had stopped at various places on the road to change mules or get refreshments, and I had experienced various kinds of treatment. In every case I had paid for the accommodation given me, but sometimes civility was great and payment small, at other times it was *vice versâ*.

Between Pretoria and Lydenburg, where the postal arrangements were precarious, welcome was more rare than further south. At the first farm at which I stopped I got some food with the members of the family, but only the dogs were civil to me. Here and elsewhere, I did all I could to show the Boers that I was friendly disposed towards them, and often they seemed to appreciate my endeavours. I was struck with their apparent great wish to have their children taught English, which did not look like any objection to British rule.

At the same time, it was borne home to me how ignorant they were of events taking place even in a neighbouring State. At one farm, where the family became quite friendly, I was told that a man who had lately stayed there, and who had just come from Zululand, had informed them that the English had been entirely beaten by the Zulus, and were all killed. All my assurances failed to convince these Boers that their information from Zululand was incorrect.

The day after my arrival at Lydenburg a patrol was organised to take me round the posts on the south-east of Sekukuni's Mountain. Major Carrington, who commanded the Volunteers in the Transvaal, and consequently was one of my most important assistants, made the arrangements for the trip. The party, all mounted, consisted of myself, Major Carrington, Mr. Steel, Financial Commissioner, Captain Knox, R.A., Captain Owen, commanding the Lydenburg mounted rifles, two orderlies, and two pack-ponies.

The first place we inspected was Kruger's Post where Mr. Glyn, a large local landowner and the Government contractor, joined us. Here there were fifteen men of Owen's corps and sixty-two Kaffirs of Eckersley's natives as a garrison. From thence we went on to Walker's Hill, where there was a similar garrison; and then to Pilgrim's Rest a former gold-digging, where we stayed the night. All along the route the farms were deserted, the houses having been burned by Sekukuni's people.

The next morning the patrol went on through some beautiful scenery to MacMac, another gold-digging, where also there was a small fort and garrison; and then we returned to Kruger's Post. The third day, having collected an escort, we marched through Doone's Kloof and over the Spekboom River to Fort Burgers.

This fort, which was in a good position on the Steelpoort River, and commanded the approaches to Sekukuni's town from the eastward, was originally built by the Dutch. It was occupied by the Volunteers in the 1876 war. When inspected it was found to be only a little ruined and quite capable of being put in order.

From the fort I could see the position of Sekukuni's town and the neighbouring hills. None of the enemy, however, put in an appearance; not even a signal fire could be traced on the horizon. Time did not allow a closer inspection from this side, and so in the evening we returned to Spekboom Fort, a work built by the English in 1878, and there we bivouacked for the night.

On August 28 we returned along the waterfall valley to Lydenburg. Here, as on the road to Pilgrim's Best, all the farms were deserted, notwithstanding the luxuriant nature of the vegetation. Oranges, lemons, sweet limes, and other tropical fruits were growing everywhere, but there were no hands to pick them. The owners and the farm labourers had fled owing to the constant raids by Sekukuni's followers.

On arrival at Lydenburg we heard that some friendly Kaffirs had been killed near Kruger's Post just after we had left it two days ago.

After a further inspection of posts occupied by small garrisons in the neighbourhood of Lydenburg, another patrol was organised to enable me to reconnoitre Sekukuni's stronghold on the west and north. The party was much as before, but pack-ponies were done away with, and such baggage as there was went in a cart by road. A start was made on August 30, and that day we reached Steencamp's Farm. It was said that the farmer here paid tribute to Mapoch, a Zulu chief who lived close by and was supposed to be neutral. The next day, starting early, we rode through a marshy plain, over a rocky pass, and off-saddled at a stream near Mapoch's *kraal*. Another halt was made on the banks of the Steelpoort River, and by evening we reached Fort Weeber, eighty-nine miles distant from Lydenburg.

This fort was at the time the headquarters of the field force that had been established for the purpose of keeping not only Sekukuni but all the surrounding country in subjection. The post itself was in good order, indicating efficient management on the part of the commanding officer, Major Carrington. But the troops suffered from want of definite orders. At the time of my inspection there were at Fort Weeber a company of the

80th Regiment, a troop of irregular horse under Captain Macaulay, a small force of artillery with Krupp and Whitworth guns, partly Volunteers and partly natives, under Captain Knox, R.A., with Captain Riedel as assistant; also, a native contingent from Rustenburg, and a few police enlisted from neighbouring friendly tribes.

As soon as I had inspected these various bodies of men, I issued such orders as seemed to me urgent for the redistribution of the forces around the Lulu Mountains, and also in regard to patrolling, the construction of forts, and sanitary arrangements in camps or hutments. On the east of the mountain, the troops, which had been scattered about in small detachments, were concentrated at Forts Burgers and Jellalabad. This enabled regular patrols to be sent out daily, and thus afforded the necessary training to men and horses. All the old posts were abolished, a few troopers only being left at Lydenburg and other stations for purposes of communication.

Before going further it may be worth mentioning that the arrangements thus made had the desired effect. The raids eastward from Sekukuni's stronghold ceased from the date of carrying out the order; and from the same date the efficiency of the mounted troops began to improve. Certain redistributions were also made for the better training of men and horses on the west side.

These orders having been sent out, and all necessary correspondence having been completed, we started again to continue our reconnaissances. The first day our party of officers and men, besides an escort of Irregulars, was quite a large one. Leaving Fort Weeber about 7.30 a.m., in two hours we reached a place where the road divided, the right going to Fort Faugh-a-Ballach and the left to Mamolobe. Taking the former, we reached a stony *koppie* opposite the Photo Pass about 11 a.m. Spreading the escort out, and advancing to the mouth of the gorge or pass, we were greeted with loud shouts and blowing of horns, and occasional firings from a party of Kaffirs among the rocks. Establishing communication with some of them, a distant conversation ensued.

From Sekukuni's side they asked what the party consisted of and what they wanted. The interpreter of the Irregulars replied that a new chief had been appointed to the command of the British forces, and that he had come with a few followers to look at the stronghold before making his arrangements to attack it. Upon this an invitation was given to me to come and fight single-handed with the Kaffir chief at that spot; and the Kaffirs added that they would abide by the issue: if *their* chief won, the reconnoitring party must go back; but if the *British* chief won, they would fall back and let the party examine the fortifications that protected that part of the mountain.

The scene was one not easily to be forgotten. On the one side, dotted among the rocks in the rugged mountain pass, the Kaffir warriors of Sekukuni, who, in their interest during the conversation, exposed themselves somewhat freely; on the other, at the entrance to the gorge, the little band of British officers; and, between the two, the Irregular horsemen who were carrying on the parley. The invitation, too, was quaint and peculiar, reminding more than one of the party of the challenge made by the Philistine giant to the advanced guard of the armies of Saul, which was accepted by the shepherd lad who eventually became King of Israel.

Perhaps a bullet from the revolver which I carried would have brought about the same result as the stone from David's sling, and laid low the challenger. But there might be treachery in the offer. Moreover I had other duty to perform, and it would not have been right to risk my life without more reason. So, the interpreter was told to say that the new chief would come again and give all the Kaffirs on the mountain plenty of opportunity to distinguish themselves. The party then continued their journey along the valley northwards, towards Fort Mamolobe, and so home.

The next day, visiting on the way a fortified *kraal* owned by Marrishane, where the people were quite friendly, we rode to Fort Oliphant, where there was a garrison of Border Horse under Captain Denison. The following day (September 5), leaving our bivouac at 5.30, we rode to Spy-Koppie, to look at the approach to Sekukuni's town from the north. And then, having made all the notes we required, and inspected the troops in the Oliphant Forts, the party separated, Major Carrington going back to Fort Weeber, while I, accompanied by Captain Knox, made my way by the bush-*veldt* road to Pretoria.

There was no loitering on the road. Three days we marched, doing fifty-three, fifty-nine, and sixty-three miles respectively, and two nights we bivouacked for a few hours, so beset by lions that we could barely, by a ring of fire, keep them off our trembling horses. On September 7 we arrived at Pretoria. It was under a month since I had left the Headquarter camp at Ulundi; and, besides inspections and other work, I had travelled by cart or on horseback over five hundred miles.

The evening I arrived I had supper with Colonel Owen Lanyon, the Administrator of the Transvaal, and then I wrote a letter, as a preliminary report, to the chief of the staff. The letter is interesting, as giving my views while the impression of what I had seen and heard was fresh upon me. It tells how I had carried out the general's instructions to be back at Pretoria between September 5 and 10; it states that there is no doubt about the inhabitants of the Lydenburg district living in daily fear of Sekukuni; and that, if British troops were withdrawn, that chief would dominate the whole country; and it winds up with the opinion that the best thing to do would be to strengthen the troops now there sufficiently to compel Sekukuni to submit.

It was estimated that one thousand British infantry, four guns, four hundred good volunteer cavalry, and a detachment of engineers, besides some two thousand natives, would be required, in addition to the force now on the spot. I asked authority to re-engage good men who were leaving the authorised corps at the front owing to their term of service having expired. Finally, I said that the administrator, to whom I had shown my proposals, considered that there was no need, because of the feeling of unrest that existed among some of the Boers, to alter in any way the disposition of troops that I had made.

Two days after the dispatch of this letter I sent my report to the chief of the staff. This consisted first of a description of my journey and of the reconnaissance that had been made of Sekukuni's stronghold; secondly, of a memorandum on the situation of affairs in the Lydenburg district, and a statement of the course that I thought ought to be adopted; and, thirdly, of a scheme of attack in case it became necessary to undertake active operations. The description has already been given in the account of my journey from Utrecht to Lydenburg and Pretoria.

Having sent off my reports, I could take no more active steps until I received instructions from the commander-in-chief. But there was a great deal to do to put in order the military administration at Headquarters.

On September 8 news was received at Pretoria that the Zulu king, Ketchwayo had been caught, with only one or two followers, in the Gnome Forest, the capture having been made by Major Marter's squadron of the King's Dragoon Guards. It was felt on all sides that this would make a complete ending of the Zulu War, and enable Sir Garnet Wolseley to arrange a final provision for the government of Zululand. I could not help wondering whether any of the staff who had come out with Sir Garnet Wolseley, but arrived too late to gain distinction in the Zulu War, would turn their eyes northward, and come up to help us in solving the problems that still required settling in the Transvaal.

Certainly, the difficulties that had always confronted British statesmen and British soldiers in South Africa from the time when the country had been handed over to the British by the original Dutch settlers, seemed all now concentrating in the Transvaal, and especially in Pretoria, where I was told to await the arrival of the general commanding.

I had previously, when many of the generals and staff were sent to England after the Battle of Ulundi, endeavoured to secure the services of an officer whom I had known well as brigade-major of cavalry in the Zulu War, and whom I thoroughly believed in, Captain Herbert Stewart. But that officer had been appointed to the staff of the Line of Communications under General Clifford. For the rest I was content to accept gladly any officer that the chief of the staff might send me.

Two immediate problems presented themselves, *viz*. preparation for a campaign against Sekukuni, which I felt sure must sooner or later take place, and guarding against risings of discontented Boers. As to the first, the principal difficulty was one of transport; as to the second, to ascertain the real feelings and aspirations of the Boer farmers. The first was entirely a military question, the second a combined civil and military one. My instructions regarding the first were that the commander-in-chief wished to avoid fighting if possible; and so, no authority had been given to make preparations. Yet, unless preparations were made *soon*, it would be impossible to undertake any active operations before the unhealthy season set in, and everything would have to be postponed for a year, if not indefinitely.

Let us see what happened, and what I did at Pretoria while I was waiting for instructions.

I had, as already stated, done my best from the time of my first appointment, not only to learn the Boers' story, but also to find out what they wanted. To this end I prosecuted inquiries in every direction, and took evidence not only from Englishmen and others who thought that the Transvaal and the Orange River State should be British colonies, but from men who thought that the Boers had good grounds for complaint, and also from Boers who thought that the country ought to be handed back to the original settlers, and formed into a Dutch Republic.

In these investigations I took an entirely different line from that taken by the administrator, Colonel Lanyon. The latter was a clever, hard-working, and courageous officer, but he held aloof on principle from those who had, as he considered, a Boer tendency, because he thought that they might influence him wrongly, and warp his judgment when he had to decide questions of difference as between the Boer and the Briton.

On September 11 there were rumours of probable risings among the Boers, but I did not think they would come to anything, partly because a good many of the inhabitants were anxious that Sekukuni's power should be destroyed, and it was easier and cheaper to have this done by the British than by themselves; and partly because the British force in the country at that time was an unusually large one.

On the 15th, accompanied by Captain Knox, I went to see Mr. Merenski, a Moravian missionary who had lived for some years in Sekukuni's territory, but afterwards had taken charge of a missionary school and colony some seven miles from Middelburg.

From this gentleman I received information that Sekukuni's main army was well armed and numbered from three to four thousand warriors. It was thought that the people's cattle were concentrated on the mountain, and that the chief would not give in without a fight. After this interview I felt more sure than ever that there would be war. I knew from experience what difficulties lay before an attacking general, especially one in command of British troops, in a country where supplies were limited, where water, except in certain localities, was scarce, and where organised transport was almost unknown.

So, directly I returned to headquarters at Pretoria, without waiting for more definite orders, I took steps to prevent the depletion by discharge of Irregular troops; I gave orders through the commissariat officer (Colonel Phillips) to fill every depot with supplies; and, most important of all, I re-engaged the Boer bullock wagons, which, with seasoned teams and experienced drivers, were returning home to their farms in the Transvaal from the Zulu War. By these measures I not only prepared quietly and steadily for a campaign against Sekukuni, but secured to the British side many Boers with their horses and cattle, and separated them, for a time at all events, from taking part in any movement against the government that might be started by disaffected countrymen of theirs.

On September 17 I received a telegram from the chief of the staff that Colonel Baker Russell, who had commanded a column in Zululand against Ketchwayo, was preparing to march to Lydenburg with the 94th Regiment, some Mounted Infantry, and some of Ferreira's Horse. The next day the telegraph line was finished to Pretoria, and I obtained authority to enrol volunteers for the Transvaal Artillery and the Border Horse.

On September 27 I rode out with the administrator of the Transvaal, who had returned to Pretoria a day or two before, to meet the Commander-in-Chief, Sir Garnet Wolseley.

A troop of Pretoria Horse headed the procession, and a squadron of the King's Dragoon Guards brought up the rear. An address, signed by some 200 inhabitants, was presented about two miles from the town. To this address Sir Garnet Wolseley made the memorable reply that 'the Vaal would run back on its course rather than the British nation retreat from any step that they had deliberately taken.' His speech, which referred to the annexation of the Transvaal, was much criticised then and since; but time has proved him right.

Sir Garnet was accompanied by General Colley, Chief of the Staff; but, owing to news received from India of the murder of Cavagnari and the British Embassy at Cabul, the latter officer had to return to India, and his place as Chief of the Staff in South Africa was assigned to Colonel Henry Brackenbury.

The day after the arrival of the commander-in-chief there was a meeting at Government House to consider the distribution of the troops and other important matters. The officers at that meeting were General George Colley, Colonel East, who had been sent from England as quartermaster-general, but was on the point of returning home, Colonel H. Brackenbury, Military Secretary, Major Clarke, R.A., an expert with natives, who knew Sekukuni and his people, and myself. The meeting was instructed to consider not only the present distribution but also what changes should be made if it became necessary to fight against Sekukuni, and also what should be the final distribution to enable law and order to be maintained in the new colony.

The result of this conference was to adopt, as far as present requirements went, and also in the case of a possible conflict with Sekukuni, the recommendations made by me in my report.

Sir Garnet Wolseley as High Commissioner South Africa

The same view of the case was also taken by the commander-in-chief, who, in a despatch to the Secretary of State for the Colonies, dated October 3, 1879, explained that he was sending Major Clarke to propose terms to Sekukuni, but that if that chief refused to submit it would not be necessary to attack his stronghold, as he could be brought to subjection by our establishing a post on his mountain, and so preventing the people from planting and the cattle from grazing.

At the meeting it also came out that, in the event of Sekukuni refusing our terms, any operations that became necessary in the Lydenburg district were to be under the immediate command of Lieut.-Colonel Baker Russell, who was then on the march from Zululand to Middelburg.

THE SEKUKUNI WAR

On September 29 Sir Garnet Wolseley was sworn in as High Commissioner of the Transvaal. The usual assemblies and dinners followed. The same day General Colley went off by post-cart to Durban, *en route* for India; and Major Clarke went to Sekukuni's country to try and treat for peace. The result of Clarke's mission, as told in the official account of the war, was briefly as follows. The conditions that were offered to Sekukuni were:—

1. He was to admit our sovereignty and pay taxes.
2. He was to be responsible for the maintenance of peace and order in his own location.
3. He was to pay a fine of 2,500 head of cattle (500 more than he had previously promised to pay).
4. He was to accept a military or police post on his mountain.

The message was sent to Sekukuni by Clarke from Fort Weeber, by the hand of two Basutos, with an explanation that it came from a great chief specially deputed by the queen to make terms with him. The messengers saw Sekukuni, who told them that Ketchwayo was not captured, and that if they came again with such messages they would be killed. However, in sending them back, he sent with them Mangakani, his mother's brother,

Moxapoxapo, an old councillor, Jim, a personal attendant, and six other men. When this party arrived at Fort Weeber on October 11, Major Clarke explained to them in detail the terms offered to Sekukuni, and sent them back with his own messengers to Sekukuni's town. Before going they asked if sheep and goats or money would be accepted in lieu of cattle, and Major Clarke obtained authority to tell them that money could be given instead of cattle at the rate of £5 per head.

On October 21 the messengers returned to Fort Weeber, saying that Sekukuni was a poor man and could not pay the fine, but that he would like Major Clarke to come to his *kraal* and talk matters over. Major Clarke declined to go until Sekukuni agreed to the terms; but once more he sent back the chief's messengers (Moxapoxapo and Jim) accompanied by three messengers, one of whom was his own servant, a man who knew Sekukuni well and had frequently been to his *kraal*. This last embassy did its best to get Sekukuni to agree to the proposed terms, modified as above mentioned, but the chief absolutely refused, saying he would never give in but would fight to the last.

While this palaver had been going on between Clarke and Sekukuni, I took up again the double task that I had started before the arrival of Headquarters, *viz*. intelligence work regarding the Boers and preparation for a possible campaign on the Lulu Mountains. In regard to the former I was much assisted by a Boer who came to call on me at this time, and became my firm friend and trusty councillor as long as I remained in the country. This Boer had fought on the British side during the late campaign; he had learned the art of war in the school of experience, and had made his mark as a leader of men.

Many were the discussions held between me and this rough soldier, how certain features of ground should be attacked or defended, or what should be done by a named force under certain assumed circumstances.

Little did either of us think at the time that the knowledge acquired by this Boer while fighting on the side of the British would ever be used against them. Many were the talks also regarding what might be the conduct of the Boers under certain political treatment, and what was the best way of governing them. It may be remarked here, that all through the various rumours and threats of risings that took place while this Boer was at Pretoria the advice, he gave me was absolutely reliable. When the Sekukuni war was over, and the Boers had for the time settled down, and I had been told that there was no more likelihood of active work, and I might return to England, I said to my friend, 'Well, F——, I suppose the Boers won't break out any more *now*?'

To which he replied, 'They won't, *commandant*, as long as *you* are here.'

'But,' said I, 'when I am gone, another *commandant* will be appointed in my place, and he will see that a sufficient force is kept up, and will arrange for their proper distribution and efficiency.'

However, he would not commit himself, and only said, 'We shall see, we shall see—if the Boers don't get their rights, and if proper military measures are not taken, they will rise against the British rule.'

But to return to our story:

On October 1, having been somewhat shaken by the unusually hard work of body and brain that I had lately undergone, I went by way of change to stay with the Administrator at Government House. While there I constantly came across the best of the British who were living at or passing through Pretoria. Among others, I met Dr. William Russell, the famous war correspondent, whom I had known in former days during the Indian Mutinies, and elsewhere.

On the 3rd the Constitution arranged by Sir Garnet Wolseley for the Government of the Transvaal appeared in the *Gazette*. There was to be an executive council of five *ex officio* members, and three elected by the Administrator. The *ex officio* ones were the Officer Commanding the troops (the Commandant), the Chief Justice (Mr. Coetzee), the Colonial Secretary, the Secretary for Foreign Affairs, and one other. The council was only to be called upon to advise when required to do so by the administrator (or governor).

I could not help feeling that this was hardly a liberal enough arrangement to meet the aspirations of the people. By it the whole power was placed in the hands of the administrator, and on him it depended in a great measure whether or not it was a success.

At this time the Boers from the country round about were assembling at Pretoria, as is their custom once in three months, to attend the Sacraments of their Church. This assembly was taken advantage of by them to discuss the political position. Consequently, by means of my friends in the town, I was able to gain a good deal of useful information. My feeling at the time was that much might be done by sympathetic treatment to win the people over and reconcile them to British rule.

The Englishmen they had usually met hitherto at gold-diggings, or even in the towns, were not of the best; and at the same time they imagined that those they met were typical of the nation. All the more was it necessary that those in authority should mix freely with the people they governed and endeavour to show them what were the thoughts and feelings towards them of English gentlemen.

On October 9, Captain Herbert Stewart, the staff officer of the General of Communications, arrived at Pretoria, and was given a table in my office. To this officer all the arrangements that were being made for a possible campaign against Sekukuni were explained. Advantage also was taken of his arrival to send the regular staff officer of the Transvaal District (Major Creagh) to Lydenburg, to settle various disputes that had arisen among the Volunteers, and to see that the orders issued from headquarters were being properly carried out.

The same day a report was received of a slight Boer disturbance at Middelburg. Some fifty Boers had interfered with the law taking effect on a man for ill-using a native. The news was brought in by Captain Raafe, who had commanded a troop of horse in the Zulu War. The distance (about ninety miles) was covered by him on one horse in eleven hours. On receipt of this news, I accompanied the administrator to a conference held by Sir Garnet Wolseley, with the result that a troop of cavalry was ordered to the disturbed town from Heidelburg, to be relieved a day or two afterwards by a company of regular infantry. The administrator also went there with his private secretary to inquire personally into the matter.

At this time (October 11) a somewhat peculiar correspondence reached me at Pretoria. It was written by the officer commanding the column that was supposed to be on the march from Zululand to the Lydenburg district, and was addressed to the senior commissariat officer. The purport was as follows:—

> Six drivers and five leaders have deserted and the force is at a standstill. This is most serious. You should take decided steps to have these deserters captured and flogged, and be very careful that they forfeit all their pay.

Fortunately, a date was added (*viz.* Intombi River, 4-10-79), which was the only useful part of the message, because it enabled a staff officer who knew the country to calculate when the column might turn up. There was no chance of catching the native drivers.

Anxious, no doubt, to a certain extent, at the delay attending the march of this column, and also of other troops that were ordered up to the Transvaal, and doubtful as to what might result any day from the seditious movements of the Boers in various parts of the country, the commander-in-chief determined to push on the preparations for a possible campaign against Sekukuni, and with that object he directed that headquarters should be moved to Middelburg. No doubt he judged that active operations against that chief would, for a time at all events, quiet the Boers; and that, if the war were carried on successfully and quickly, he would have a large force available for any eventualities.

In order to make the necessary arrangements I shifted my office from Government House to a central hotel, where I could personally direct all movements. Here Captain Stewart worked with me; but not for long, because it was thought necessary to take him away from the Line of Communications, and attach him as Staff Officer to Colonel Baker Russell, where his great zeal and natural abilities, and the knowledge he had gained, while at Pretoria, of the whole situation, would be invaluable in enabling the expedition to be carried out with the best chance of success.

On October 17 the commander-in-chief held a review of the few troops left in Pretoria, and the next day he took his departure, accompanied by Colonel Brackenbury, Dr. Jackson, Mr. Herbert, and Major MacCalmont, to personally superintend the operations in the Lydenburg district.

For a time, until Colonel Lanyon returned, I was in sole civil and military charge at Pretoria. This town was not only the centre of government, but also the advanced base of supplies and organisation for the forces collecting round Sekukuni's country, and the depot where military stores were looked over and sorted. The garrison at the time was extraordinarily weak, only one troop of Regular Cavalry (King's Dragoon Guards), and the Headquarters and one company of the 80th Foot. The 21st regiment, which had been destined for Pretoria and was on the way there, was diverted to Middelburg.

Before headquarters left, the chief of the staff and I went through together the commissariat arrangements for the troops that were going to be employed at the front and on the lines of communication if war took place. This was no doubt a judicious thing to do; but, as before stated, unless I had made preparations steadily and incessantly from the time when I arrived in the country, and especially if I had not secured the Boer ox-wagons returning from the Zulu War, the necessary supplies for the forces detailed for the attack on Sekukuni's stronghold could not have been collected until after the wet season—that is to say, for another year.

Even as it was, there was great difficulty in making the arrangements because of the lack of energy on the part of some of the contractors and others concerned, and because of the frequent changes that were made in the detail of troops sent to the front. From the time when headquarters left Pretoria the chief of the staff and I kept up a running correspondence. The letters of the former were taken up for the most part with demands for stores, mine with statements of what could be done locally to comply with the demands.

But, although supplying the force that was concentrating at Middelburg and in the Lydenburg district was an urgent matter, it was not so critical at the time we are dealing with (the latter part of October) as the hostile movements of a portion of the Boer community. Had these movements been allowed to continue, and had any real outbreak taken place, the troops operating against Sekukuni would have been cut off from supplies, and the position would have been a critical one. No sooner had Sir Garnet Wolseley established his Headquarters at Middelburg, than rumours of threatened Boer attacks and proposed concentrations 'in *laager*' came in from all sides.

But, with his usual determination and courage, once having made up his mind to carry on war against Sekukuni, nothing would divert him from his purpose. He had placed me at Pretoria in military command, and he left me, in concert with the administrator, to protect the country in his rear, in the full assurance that the best would be done, whatever turned up. No wonder those who served under such a general did so gladly and loyally.

Among the dangers that threatened British rule in the Transvaal from disaffected Boers, one of the most serious was a scheme to attack Pretoria. The news of this reached me while in church on the 26th instant. The circumstances were somewhat sensational. The Bishop of Pretoria (Dr. Bousfield), an eloquent preacher, was in the middle of his morning discourse at the cathedral. I was one of the congregation, and was sitting just opposite the pulpit. The interest in the sermon was so great that you might have heard a pin drop, when the sound of an approaching horseman mingled with the preacher's words. The times were exciting ones, nearly everyone in that church was expecting news of some sort or another.

The horseman was heard to dismount at the western door and to enter the cathedral. After a glance to see where I was sitting, he marched up the aisle, his spurs and sword clanking as he went along. Evidently, he had travelled far and fast to deliver his message. The bishop stopped his sermon. I took from the messenger the despatch that he was carrying, glanced at it, put it in my pocket, and motioned to the preacher to continue his discourse. The congregation naturally thought that the message was not of much importance, and settled down to hear the rest of the sermon. But they were deceived. The message came from headquarters, and intimated that most reliable information had been received to the effect that the Boers intended making an attack on Pretoria the following night.

Now, as has before been said, I had friends among the Boers and had already been warned of possible attacks, and had made all necessary arrangements to guard against them. But I could not help, during the rest of the sermon, thinking more of my plans than of the preacher's words; and, when service was over, I went round the different posts in the town to see that all my officers knew their orders and were on the alert. Whether or not those who led the Boers had an inkling that their plans were discovered, I do not know, but the attack on Pretoria did not take place.

There were, however, other movements in the Transvaal that showed considerable unrest, if nothing else. For instance, reports were received on the 27th that some Boers had been taking ammunition from a general store at Potchefstrom—about forty of them going in at a time and taking it without the legal permits, but putting the price of it on the counter. Also, that Boers were collecting at Christian Pretorius's farm, with the object of attacking Standerton.

In addition to these reports, further rumours were received that the Boers were collecting in Pretoria with the object of 'a demonstration,' if not an attack that very night. All possible arrangements having been made, I could do nothing more. But during that night I walked to the barracks to caution the commanding officer there, and I also again visited the posts in the town, where all was quiet except for some glee-singing in one of the houses.

Till quite a late hour I wrote letters and drafts of orders in my room at the hotel; and then, hot and tired, I opened the glass door for another breath of fresh air and another turn in the moonlight. Stepping out, without precaution, I stumbled and nearly fell over something lying on the doorsill, and found that it was my Zulu boy 'Malinder,' who, with rifle and ammunition, and wrapped in a large barrack blanket, had stationed himself there because he had heard that the Boers were going to make an attack that night, and he wished 'to take care of master.' But even he had gone to sleep on that particular evening.

The morning of the 28th broke without any attack. But the rumours of disturbances were as plentiful as ever. That day I had a long talk with the field-cornet from Heidelburg, and gathered that the Boers' chief grievance at that time was a sentimental one, but that several acts by the government had much irritated them the last few months, such as restrictions on the sale of ammunition, &c.

By the end of the month, after careful consideration of the whole matter, I came to the conclusion that something more than local precautions were necessary against possible Boer risings; and so, acting on the authority that I had received from the commander-in-chief, I set on foot a movement of troops up country, to strengthen the force at Pretoria, without weakening the garrison of any fortified post on the lines of communication between that place and Natal.

Then, when all was arranged, I managed through an influential friend to hold a secret conference with the wire-puller of the Boers who at that time was in Pretoria. Over coffee and pipes we held a prolonged discussion which lasted well into the night. The friend acted as interpreter, when it was needed, and the conversation was practically as follows:—

Commandant: 'What is the meaning of the various movements of Boers which are taking place throughout the country?'

Wire-puller: 'The people are not satisfied with the way they are being treated by the British Government in the Transvaal, and they want their independence.'

Commandant: 'But was it not the case that, when Shepstone came to Pretoria, with nothing more than an escort of policemen, the great majority of the people were in favour of the country being handed over to the British?'

Wire-puller: 'Maybe. But those who voted were not really representative of the country. Many farmers in far-off places never had a chance of giving an opinion in the matter.'

Commandant: 'We can't go into that now. Let us consider the present situation. Would the majority of the people be contented to live under the British flag if they were given a fair amount of self-government?'

Wire-puller: 'It is difficult to say. There are many shades of opinion. Some, no doubt, would prefer the British flag, others would never be content except with a pure Dutch Republic; but a good many are wavering, and would be influenced by the amount of self-government granted to them, and also by the way in which they are treated by those in authority.'

Commandant: 'Assuming that those who are discontented cannot be pacified, what will they do?'

Wire-puller: 'We are getting on dangerous ground. As you know, nearly all the British troops have been concentrated in Sekukuni's country. Suppose a number of young Boer farmers were to "form *laager*" between those troops and Pretoria, and cut off all supplies?'

Commandant: 'I should march against the *laager* and destroy it.'

Wire-puller: 'But, from our experience of British troops in the Zulu War, many of the regiments are made up of boys, quite untrained in the art of war, and not to be compared in shooting power with our hardy farmers.'

Commandant: 'No doubt you are referring to the British Infantry, but if I had to march against a Boer *laager* I should use Cavalry and Artillery.'

Wire-puller (quickly): 'But you have none of those troops here, and telegraph lines can be cut.'

Commandant: 'They are on their way, some will be here tomorrow; I am satisfied that I have at hand enough for my purpose. The Boer farmers may be good and brave—I believe they are. They may have wrongs, some imaginary and some real; I sympathise with them. I would, if I had the power, give them as free a hand as possible in the management of the affairs of the country that they occupy.

'But I am a British officer, serving under a British general who is now employed at the Lulu Mountains in subduing the common enemy of Boer and Briton, and if any hostile gathering takes place which might in any way endanger the success of Sir Garnet Wolseley's work, I am prepared to attack it, and, I believe, to beat it. The Boers have no guns and no organised cavalry. I could bombard their *laager* from a distance, and if their horsemen attacked my guns, I could ride them down with my cavalry. Moreover, if they break out in open rebellion against the flag that they have already acknowledged, the grant to them of self-government would, no doubt, be postponed indefinitely.'

The Boer leader was evidently impressed, not only with what I said, but with the confidence that I showed in the troops coming up country to put down any risings that might take place on the part of the Boers. My friend also, besides interpreting, supplemented the arguments with advice of his own.

When the Boer wire-puller had gone away, and I and my friend were left alone, we came to the conclusion that orders for an attack on Pretoria would not for the present be issued. And we were right. Sir Garnet Wolseley was freed from any immediate danger of an attack on the most important station of his line of communications, and could do what he liked in Sekukuni's country.

Let us now turn to the field operations, and briefly recount what took place in the theatre of war from the time when Sir Garnet Wolseley and his Staff established Headquarters at Middelburg on October 18, until he returned to Pretoria on December 9, 1879.

On October 21 Colonel Baker Russell's column reached

Middelburg from Lake Chrissie. The same day the 21st Fusiliers, under the guidance of Herbert Stewart, arrived from Heidelburg. Colonel Baker Russell was put in command of the forces, which consisted of a troop of regular Cavalry, a detachment of Mounted Infantry, some Irregular Horse, two 7-pdr. guns, a detachment of Royal Engineers, and two battalions of Infantry.

On the 24th the greater part of this force marched for Fort Weeber, and on the 25th was followed by Army Headquarters. By this time Sir Garnet Wolseley knew that Major Clarke had failed to persuade Sekukuni to give in, and that thus there was no alternative but war. So, he took the necessary steps to concentrate the troops for the campaign, and arrange for their supplies of food and ammunition. Among his measures was one instructing Captain MacLeod to bring a Swazi contingent to Burgers Post.

Headquarters arrived at Fort Weeber on the 28th, and, on investigating the state of supplies there, it was found that the amounts were far below what had been anticipated, especially in regard to meat and forage. Urgent representations on the subject were made to the General of Communications at Pietermaritzburg and to me at Pretoria. But stores were on the road. The General Commanding (Sir Garnet Wolseley) also made a reconnaissance in the direction of Mamolobe's Mountain, to get an idea of the nature of the mountains, and of the difficulties attending an advance from the western side. Having then obtained all the information they could give him regarding the situation from Major Carrington, commanding the troops on the spot, and Major Clarke, the political officer, he decided upon his plan of operations.

Establishing a post on the Lulu Mountains, which had hitherto been adopted as the measure to be taken if Sekukuni refused to accede to terms, would at the best be only a preliminary operation, and the result it brought about might take some time to realise; whereas a direct attack on the stronghold itself from the north would, if successful, end the war by one blow. Under the circumstances of the delay that had occurred in bringing reinforcements to the theatre of operations, and of the hostile movements of discontented Boers, rapid action was very important.

So, the commander-in-chief decided to follow the latter course, and, transferring his advanced post from Fort Weeber to Mapashlela's Drift, to make his main attack by the entrance to the valley in which Sekukuni's town was situated. This being settled, the line of supply from Pretoria was shifted along the bush veldt road to Fort Oliphants, the line from Wakkerstrom through Middelburg still continuing to supply Lydenburg and Fort Oliphants through Fort Weeber. A force based on Fort Burgers and Lydenburg was to attack from the heights east of the town simultaneously with the attack of the main body in the valley. With the Lydenburg force would be the Swazis.

It will not, I think, be necessary to go into details regarding the assembly and organisation of the little army of Regulars and Colonials and Native Levies that were collected by Sir Garnet Wolseley for the attack on Sekukuni. It will give an idea of the magnitude of the business if I say that, according to the monthly returns signed by me as head of all the troops in the Transvaal, there were in September 3,020 men and 866 horses; in October 4,140 men and 800 horses; in November 4,630 men and 1,295 horses; and in December some 16,000 men and 1,300 horses. This included the force detailed for the Sekukuni campaign.

On November 11 Sir Garnet, writing from Fort Weeber, informed the Secretary of State for War of his plans (as already briefly described), and indicated some of the difficulties of the situation.

The operations were being undertaken at a distance of more than 500 miles from the sea base at Durban. The nearest farmhouse was fifty miles off, and no supplies could be purchased within 100 miles. Pretoria and Wakkerstrom, the depots whence supplies were sent, were 150 and 230 miles distant, and fifty more had to be covered to reach Mapashlela's Drift. The lines of communication had to be guarded as if in an enemy's country in consequence of the hostile attitude of some of the Boers.

At the same date as this despatch, orders were issued for a

further movement of troops on the line of communications, with a view of strengthening the position at Pretoria; and I, as *commandant*, was given power to order up troops from the Utrecht district, as well as from anywhere else in the Transvaal, if I thought it necessary.

By November 23 the state of supplies enabled a concentration to be made of troops for the attack on Sekukuni's town as already arranged. On the 24th the Water Koppie was occupied, and on the 28th the stronghold was stormed. The following report was sent by special messenger to Pretoria the next day, and telegraphed from there to the Cape and England:—

Headquarters, Sekukuni's Town, November 29.—
Baker Russell's column encamped before this place yesterday, as previously planned. Arrangements made for simultaneous attack this morning from both sides of the mountain. At daybreak the attack commenced. Ferreira led the right attack, and took Sekukuni's own *kraal*, from the heights to the south. Colonel Murray commanded central attack with detachment Royal Engineers, 21st Fusiliers, 94th Regiment, detachment 80th Regiment, four guns Transvaal Artillery, and Rustenburg contingent. . . .
This attack was chiefly directed on the fighting *koppie*. Major Carrington led the left attack with Mounted Infantry, Border Horse, Transvaal Mounted Rifles, and Zoutspansberg native contingent. He captured the lower town, and cleared the hills above, sweeping round to Sekukuni's own *kraal*. About seven o'clock the Swazis appeared on the hills above, having fought their way up from the eastward of the town; and, most of the caves having been cleared and burnt, at ten o'clock the fighting *koppie* was stormed. All the corps took part in the assault, which was completely successful. Fighting *koppie* and town now in our hands.

On December 2 Sekukuni, who had hidden in a cave at the top of the mountain, surrendered to Ferreira. Orders were then issued to break up the field force, and distribute the regular troops at Lydenburg and elsewhere.

Headquarters, with Sekukuni as prisoner, returned to Pretoria, where they arrived on December 9.

The day of arrival was marked by as much ceremony as Pretoria and its scratch garrison could provide. Sekukuni did the last part of the journey in state in a mule-wagon. A squadron of the King's Dragoon Guards supplied the escort. The chief, who had a wretched worn-out look, sat on a box in the centre of the wagon with a skin round him. His appearance was hardly up to expectation, for he was supposed to be the cleverest native in South Africa. Two *indunas* were with him, and a wife and one or two children. After lodging the chief in the jail, an address of congratulation was presented to Sir Garnet, the guard of honour on the occasion consisting of a company of the 4th King's Own Infantry, the band of the 80th Regiment, and a squadron King's Dragoon Guards. Nearly all Pretoria turned out for the double event.

On December 11 there was a review of all the troops before the commander-in-chief. The total on parade amounted to 1625 men, 392 horses, and six guns.

This was a large force for the protection of the capital, if it is compared with the one considered suffcient two months earlier, when the Sekukini expedition was in full swing. Moreover it was largely increased by troops coming south when that war was over.

SEKUKUNI AND FAMILY IN 1880.
When prisoners at Pretoria.

Bindon Blood

Zulu War Experiences
By Sir Bindon Blood

Directly after I left India, trouble had broken out with Afghanistan, which led to the commencement of the Second Afghan War in October 1878. I of course was anxious to go back and join in, but I found that under the regulations I had to serve three years at home before I could be sent to India again. This was unlucky, but as there was no help for it, I accepted the situation and settled down at Chatham, enjoying the available hunting and shooting, meeting many old friends and making some new ones. So, the time passed until, at the end of January 1879, news of the disaster at Isandhlwana in Zululand arrived one morning, and I went to the War Office by the next train to see our D.A.G. about it. When I appeared he told me I was already in orders for Zululand with my company of the Royal Engineers, and that I was to move to Aldershot with it at once to mobilise, which I did in due course.

We were brought up to war strength very quickly and satisfactorily by the transfer to us of men from other companies of the corps, who, as it was 'all in the family,' gave us of their best, so that we started officers and men a truly united and efficient lot, every man determined to do his best. I have before me a longish official letter addressed after the end of the campaign to the officer then in command of the company, and setting forth the authorities' strong approval of the company and of its work during the operations. So that our confident hopes at starting were—if I may put it so—justified as usual.

But the mobilisation of the rest of the force that went to Zululand in 1879, the infantry especially, was not so satisfactory.

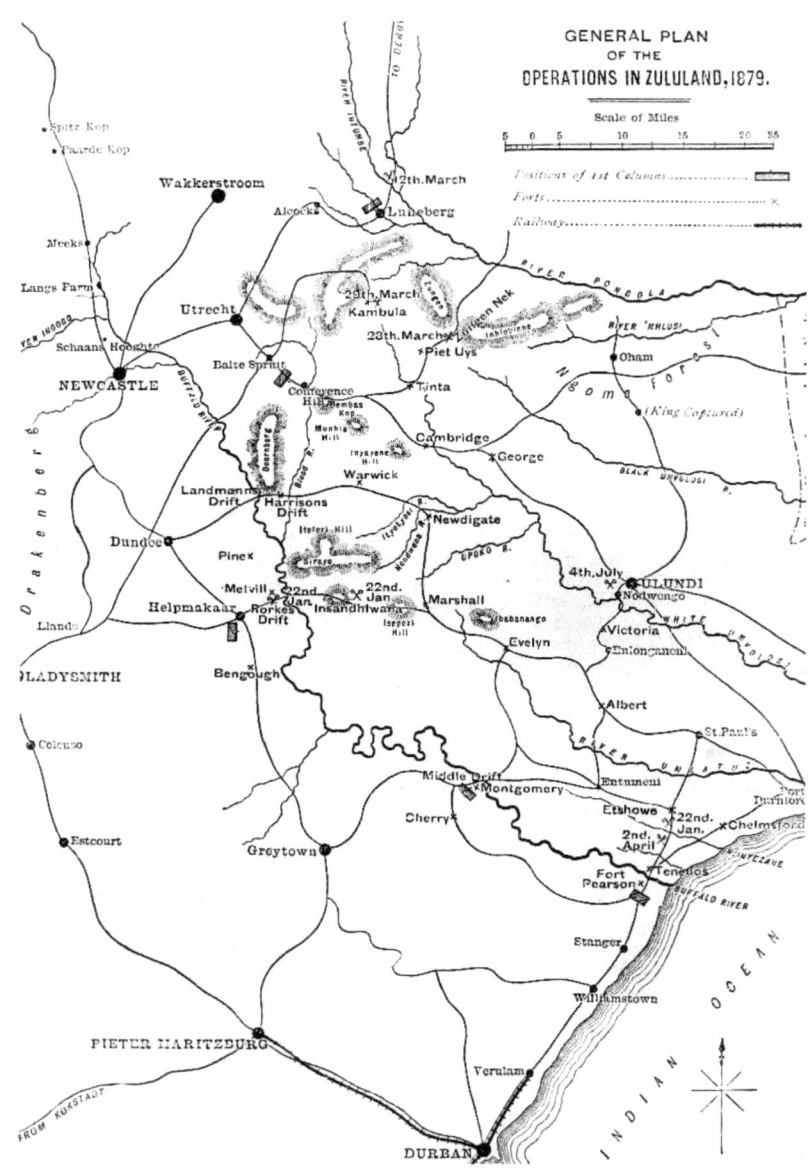

The battalions all required large drafts to bring them up to war strength, and in this case the drafts were provided by transfers from other corps, which were already short of trained men and could not part with them. Thus, it came about that our battalions landed in Zululand full of incompletely trained men, a great proportion of whom had never fired a round of ball cartridge, while many had never fired a round of blank, before they embarked.

I put it thus because great trouble was taken on the voyage in the instruction of the recruits on board the transports, so that in the harbour at St.Vincent for instance, where our ship anchored for about twenty-four hours, the bullets were frequently heard singing somewhat unduly near our ears! And the same thing happened also at Simon's Bay, where, owing to bungling about coal, we wasted nearly a week. Our ship, and I believe most if not all of those carrying men and horses, were despatched remarkably quickly from England, but with such short supplies of coal that many days were wasted in coaling them on the voyage, at St.Vincent and Simon's Bay.

In the case of our ship, according to our skipper, if twelve hours extra had been spent in coaling at Portsmouth before our start, we should have saved one day at St.Vincent and nearly six at Simon's Bay, which we spent over coaling on the outward voyage; or nearly six days 'net' in time, besides considerable extra cost of coal. And moreover, the extra twelve hours at Portsmouth could have provided coal for our ship's return voyage, thus saving another considerable sum of money on account of time and cost of coal. I believe that much the same thing happened to many or most of the transports in this expedition.

At St.Vincent we and our horses were inspected by the general commanding the cavalry of the expedition, a man universally liked and believed in, but without experience of active service. I had a slight acquaintance with him and he invited me to go with him to see some of the other transports lying in the harbour that were carrying mounted troops.

The first ship we came to had on board the headquarters and several troops of the famous 'Death or Glory Boys,' many of whom I knew. Just before this regiment had embarked, an unfortunate accident happened to their newly appointed commanding officer—a fine soldier—which prevented his embarking, and so the previous colonel was brought back *pro tem*. He was a first-class man, being soon afterwards promoted to major-general, and he was also a bit of a character. Now in those days on embarking with troops we used to be served out—I think *gratis*—with a suit of 'sea kit,' coat and trousers, of stout naval serge, and a knitted cap, the same for all ranks. So, when our cavalry general and I with his staff, boarded the nearest transport, we saw a smallish man in sea kit hurrying up to us, who saluted the general. The general shook hands with him and said, 'Why ——, I quite thought you were one of the men!'

'So I am, Sir—so I am!' replied the colonel.

When the general said, 'Just the right answer, my dear ——, to my stupid remark!'—very neat on both sides, as we thought!

At last, we arrived at Durban and disembarked, with our 60 or 70 horses alive, but quite unfit for anything but rest and careful exercising during the next fortnight or more. We managed to get some mules and country horses locally, and started for our division, which was encamped at the mouth of the Tugela, about 60 miles to the north of Durban.

I was left at Durban to arrange for materials for a bridge over the Tugela near our divisional camp. This took several days, during which the King's Dragoon Guards and. 17th Lancers arrived, dressed for the campaign in their tunics and booted overalls and gold lace all complete, except that Sam Browne sword-belts had been imposed upon the officers, making them feel, as an old friend in the 17th said to me, 'Like a lot of damned tenors in an opera!'

At this time the prince imperial arrived, and I was presented to him. He had a charming manner, was very well informed and most promising as a soldier. He was also greatly interested in India, and I had several pleasant conversations with him about that country.

Durban in 1879 a pretty little place consisting of a square and two or three streets near the sea, with some picturesque houses

Prince Impérial, 1878

and country roads on the Berea, a ridge running along a mile or so from the sea and parallel to it. It was said to be hot in the summer, something like Bombay, but in the end of February and beginning of March we did not find it unpleasant. I was of course in camp with my company until it left, and then I stayed in a hotel where I was all right and enjoyed meeting many interesting and pleasant people.

As soon as I had finished the special work for which I had stayed behind at Durban, I started off at daylight one morning on horse-back, with my soldier groom on another horse leading a third which carried our kit; intending to get to our division on the second day, doing about 45 miles the first day and 15 or so on the second. It was a pleasant ride on an unmetalled track, through cultivated country and scattered trees. We crossed several shallow rivers with clear rapid streams and we rode through some picturesque villages with cottages covered by flowering creepers and gardens full of flowers. I specially remember one near Durban that was called by the famous name of Verulam.

We found an inn with breakfast at a suitable hour, and sat down to good plain food at a long table presided over by our hostess, who had a favouring eye for a soldier and put me beside her! On my other side was a pretty girl who was one of a party of four, made up by another girl and two men, travelling in an American 'spider' with a team of four nice horses that had passed us on the road. So, I had a pleasant breakfast and the young lady was so kind as to say she hoped to see me again later on at dinner.

Accordingly, we saddled up and went on by a bridlepath—a short cut—so that we did not see the spider party again until we halted in a good-sized village for dinner, at which I again found myself next to the same young lady, to whom of course I proceeded to make myself as agreeable as possible. All went well until it was time to part, and I began some nonsense in the way of goodbye, when I noticed that the man on the other side of the young lady seemed uneasy, and presently said something that I did not quite catch. I asked if he had addressed me, and he observed that he had, and that if he had me outside, he would do something or other, I forget exactly what.

So, I said I should be very glad to oblige him in any way, and we adjourned outside. There it became clear that he wanted a round or two with fists, to which I was quite agreeable, and calling up my hefty sapper groom, I gave him my coat to hold, and was ready for my friend, who was a bit bigger than I was, but clumsy-looking. It turned out that he was a duffer with his fists, and that as long as I did not allow him to close, he was in my hands; so I did not hurt him, and the matter ended amicably in a few minutes. I was informed afterwards that my adversary had been doing time in jail for selling guns to the Zulus, that he was on his way home therefrom when I met him, and that the young lady I had been talking to was engaged to him.

Next day I arrived at the headquarters of the 1st Division, Zulu Field Force, of which I had been appointed Commanding Royal Engineer.

The Amazulu

The Amazulu—the 'Celestials'—commonly called the Zulus, were an unimportant tribe until the early years of the nineteenth century. At that time, they inhabited the pleasant and fertile country in the north-east of what is now Zululand, about the Black and White Umvolosi Rivers, and seem to have been chiefly known as producers and peddlers of tobacco. About *A.D.* 1800 they were ruled by a chief who had a nephew named Utshaka—'Daybreak'—commonly called Chaka; and this nephew having managed to collect a following, killed his uncle the chief, took his place, and organised the fighting men of the tribe in a few years into the most formidable native army in South Africa.

With this army, before 1830, Chaka occupied the whole of what is now Zululand, and also took possession of the territory that is now Natal, exterminating or driving out the previous inhabitants of both areas as he proceeded. In Natal he first came in contact with white men, 'Boers' from the Cape Colony, which we had taken from the Dutch, and from which there was an extensive migration of Boers to the interior, commencing about 1825, followed by the formation of the states which are now included in the Union of South Africa.

But Chaka saw little of this, as his oppressive rule had aroused discontent, so that his younger brother Dingaan—the 'Poor Creature'—murdered him about 1830 and took his place. Dingaan attacked the Natal colonists at once, destroyed Durban, and was also guilty of more than one treacherous massacre. But he was defeated ultimately in 1840 by a rising of Zulus under his younger brother Panda, assisted by 400 mounted Boers; and thereupon he took refuge with a small tribe near Delagoa Bay, who promptly murdered him to curry favour with his pursuers.

After this, on the 14th February 1840, the Natal Boers proclaimed Panda King of the Zulus, and also declared their own sovereignty over Natal. Then, after some fighting, the British Government occupied Natal in 1842, and that Colony settled down under the consequent reign of law and order.

Panda reigned over the Zulus until his death in 1872, when he was succeeded by his son Ketchwayo. Ketchwayo added to the efficiency of the Zulu Army in various ways, but specially by acquiring for it a large proportion of rifles, which he was foolishly permitted to do; and before long it became evident that he had made up his mind to try conclusions with the white men, and that his army and most of his subjects were at one with him about this.

Accordingly, our relations with Ketchwayo soon became strained. Many unpleasant occurrences took place and insolent replies were received to reasonable and just requests on several occasions up to 1878, when the climax was reached. In July of that year a body of armed Zulus entered Natal territory, took two refugee Zulu women out of the huts of British subjects, and killed them when they had conveyed them into Zulu territory which was near. When remonstrances and demands were sent to the Zulu King, insolent replies were returned; and when a final message was sent to Ketchwayo, demanding, *inter alia*, the surrender of the men who had violated British territory, no satisfactory reply was received; and so, on the 4th January 1879, Her Majesty's High Commissioner, Sir Bartle Frere, placed the enforcement of all demands in the hands of Lieut.-General Lord

Chelmsford, who commanded the troops in South Africa,

Lord Chelmsford was originally a Guardsman, and in the days of the "extra rank," when captains in the Guards ranked as lieut.-colonels and lieutenants as captains, he exchanged while comparatively a young man to command a line battalion. He was adjutant-general in India when I first met him, being universally liked and respected, and considered one of the best adjutant-generals there had ever been.

The forces at Lord Chelmsford's disposal at the front were as under, the numbers given being close approximations, namely:

British Infantry, with 200 Naval Brigade, (2 gatlings)	5,800
White mounted troops	750
R.E. one company	120
Natives on foot	9,000
" mounted	250
Guns 7 pdr. on wheels	8
Rocket tubes	2

This force was divided into four 'columns,' three of them being of about 2,000 white men each, and the fourth of about 3,500 natives; the 1st column, under Colonel Pearson of the Buffs, at the mouth of the Tugela; the 4th under Colonel Evelyn Wood, V.C., in front of Utrecht; the 3rd under Colonel Glyn about Helpmakaar and Rorke's Drift; and the 2nd under Colonel Durnford to the south of the 3rd, on the strong position called Kranz Kop.

Ketchwayo's army was said to amount to some 40,000 efficient men, all foot-soldiers trained to fight at close quarters with the stabbing *assegai* and ox-hide shield. They had been lately equipped with a considerable proportion of rifles, including many breech-loaders of different patterns, but fortunately for us had no idea of the tactical methods and arrangements required to make long-range fire-arms useful. It was generally believed that some 20.000 of Ketchwayo's army watched Lord Chelmsford's 3rd column, that the large part of the rest lay towards the mouth of the Tugela about Etshowe, and that some 5,000 or

6.000 watched Colonel Evelyn Wood's command the 4th British column.

Now perhaps it will be interesting if we devote a page or two to considering the composition and capabilities of these two forces.

The Zulu Army as I have stated was a body of infantry trained to fight hand to hand with the stabbing *assegai* and ox-hide shield. The men were little encumbered by clothing or equipment, and were very active and capable of rapid movement. Also, they were kept in good condition, and were excellent marchers and hill climbers, and they were full of courage and enthusiasm.

Of late years considerable numbers of rifles of various descriptions had been acquired and issued to the Zulu Army, but it had not taken to them, and very few of the men could shoot at all well, while the leaders had no idea of the tactics which have to be adopted with fire-arms, in order to develop their powers fully. Thus, the Zulus' idea of a normal attack was to advance in masses in crescent formation, to get close to the enemy, and then to charge home, enveloping him as far as possible. In cases where there was cover close up to a negligent enemy, and other special circumstances favoured the Zulus, these tactics succeeded. But it was very different when the force attacked was properly composed and handled, so as to give effect to the power of destroying mass formations which is possessed by modern rifles in the hands of well-trained men, and to the capabilities of artillery and cavalry. And similarly, it was repeatedly proved that Zulu forces were helpless against fortified positions, even when they were fortified in the most elementary manner.

I always understood that the Zulus managed with a minimum of transport, and that what they had was arranged on the 'coolie' system, men being utilised for it who had not come up to the physical standards of their regiments, and also women to some extent.

Turning to the British Army, we find that the six battalions in it of British infantry were an excellent lot of men. They had all been some time in South Africa and so had not been affected, like our newly mobilised troops, by the short-service-and-reserve system lately introduced in England. Their officers were of the well-known sort, who could be depended upon to lead their men anywhere. Under an absurdly mistaken idea that the South African country was too difficult for field artillery. Lord Chelmsford had only 7 pdr. mountain guns on light carriages, and very few of them—only eight in all—for a force liable to be attacked at any time by concentrations of 20,000 foot-soldiers, working in mass formations and full of courage and enthusiasm. This of course was due to remarkable ignorance in high places of the powers and capabilities of artillery.

Again, in Lord Chelmsford's army there was equal neglect of cavalry. Lord Chelmsford had, it is true, seven or eight hundred mounted men, all gallant volunteers in small bodies fit for anything that small bodies could do, but useless for such an enterprise as, say, the destruction of a Zulu mass by the operation of all the arms of the service in due combination, on any sort of suitable ground. In such a case what could the Zulus have done, practically having no firearms, absolutely no artillery, no cavalry, nothing but trumpery assegais four feet long or so, with leather shields that would only have been in their way?

Of course, Lord Chelmsford's mounted men might easily have been made into six or seven squadrons of splendid cavalry, if he had had cavalry officers fit to teach and handle them. But nothing of the sort was ever thought of.

The British force was organised in columns, the normal brigades and divisions having been entirely given up. To my mind this was a great mistake, as a complete change of organisation on starting on active service cannot be sound. Ever since I have been in the British service it has been the regular practice to organise armies anew in brigades and divisions, etc., when they are mobilised, and to furnish them with staffs newly put together for the occasion. I have always regarded this practice as one of the chief causes of the many 'regrettable occurrences' that have taken place in our campaigns.

There is no doubt that the art of field fortification might have been utilised in Natal and Zululand with much advantage, both for the defence of the Natal border, and on the lines of communication at such positions as Rorke's Drift and Isandhlwana; and consequently, it was strange that there was only one weak company of engineers with Lord Chelmsford's force, and that it was not with the column designated for the main advance. It is conceivable that if it had been with that column, the placing of the positions of Isandhlwana and Rorke's Drift in a state of defence might have been thought of, and the history of South Africa in 1879 might then have been quite different from what it was.

But the greatest defect in the composition of Lord Chelmsford's army was the utter unsuitability of its transport. This consisted practically altogether of ox-wagons, which were very cleverly constructed four-wheel vehicles, each drawn by six or eight pairs of fine oxen and requiring the services of two men. These vehicles and their draught arrangements had been evolved to meet the requirements of colonial life in South Africa, and were admirably well adapted thereto. Those requirements never made it necessary, as field service requirements do, for *great masses of transport to move and camp together*, and so to make the feeding of the consequent enormous number of bullocks an actual impossibility; as the only possible mode of feeding them was to graze them for five or six hours of daylight each day on suitable grass.

Our officers did their best to get over this difficulty, but it will easily be understood that their efforts were vain, owing to the great numbers of animals involved, and that the long delays and some of the other regrettable occurrences of the Zulu War were the inevitable result. (After Isandhlwana, great efforts were made to bring mules to Zululand from various parts of the world, and they were very useful in the final advance on Ulundi.)

Lord Chelmsford advanced into Zululand with the 3rd Column on the 11th January 1879, and soon realised that it was impossible for him with his transport and supply arrangements as they were, to make a rapid march at that season into the middle of the Zulu country. He therefore decided to move all his columns a short distance forward only, and apparently, then to await events. Accordingly, on the 20th January the 3rd Column was encamped at Isandhlwana, and next day a force of native police and mounted volunteers was sent some fourteen miles out to feel for the enemy, and reported the presence of Zulus in considerable strength.

At daylight on the 22nd a battalion of British Infantry, the Mounted Infantry and four guns started to re-enforce the troops reconnoitring, the commander-in-chief accompanying them; whilst Colonel Durnford, with the 2nd column, having been ordered out to Isandhlwana, was on the way. Meanwhile, in the night of the 21st/22nd, 20,000 Zulus moved undiscovered to within about one and a half miles of Isandhlwana Camp, which had not been put in a state of defence. In the course of the morning the Zulus attacked the camp and captured it with ease in an hour, killing about 800 white officers and men and great numbers of natives, soldiers and others; and capturing the guns, rocket-tubes, stores of ammunition, etc., together with the transport cattle, wagons and everything else.

A large number of the Zulus pursued the fugitives for a long distance, and a considerable detachment went to attack Rorke's Drift, which had not been made into a defensible post, but was strengthened by means of biscuit boxes, mealie bags and so forth, as soon as fugitives brought news of the disaster at Isandhlwana. The defenders were 139 of all ranks in number, of whom 33 were patients in hospital, and their losses were 25 killed and wounded in the defence, which was completely successful, although in the course of the night some buildings were evacuated and burnt which had been held at first. The officer in command was Lieut. Chard, R.E., and he was ably assisted by Lieut. Bromhead of the 24th Regt. and the Rev. Mr. Smith, one of the military chaplains who happened to be at the post.

The defence of Rorke's Drift post was, of course, a most remarkable exemplification of the helplessness of the Zulu Army against the most trumpery fortification, owing to their deficiency of fire-arms big and little, and this though it was composed of some of the finest fighting men to be found anywhere!

While the events described above were in progress, part of No. 1 Column comprising about 1,200 British troops under Colonel Pearson of the Buffs, having crossed the Tugela by the lower drift near the sea, proceeded on the 18th January towards Etshowe about 30 miles distant. Their progress was slow, owing to transport difficulties, and on the 22nd January, the day of Isandhlwana, they were attacked on the line of march, near the Inyezane River, by about 5,000 Zulus who had been lying in wait for them. After an action lasting one and a half hours, in which all arms were brought into play by the British commander, the Zulus were defeated and put to flight, and the British column marched on to its bivouac, about three miles from the field of battle. The British loss was 10 killed and 16 wounded, while over 300 Zulus were slain. The Zulus made considerable use of fire-arms in this action, but ineffectually of course owing to want of training.

The day after the action the column reached and occupied the position at Etshowe, with the intention of making it a base for the further advance on Ulundi, but on the 29th news arrived of the disaster at Isandhlwana. Thereupon Colonel Pearson decided to hold on to Etshowe with about 1,300 white and 60 native fighting men, and to send all the mounted men and spare natives back to the Tugela. By the 10th February the fort was completed on a sound scheme, in a most creditable manner, by the company of engineers in the garrison, ably assisted by the other soldiers and sailors, all under the orders of that brave and able commander, Colonel Pearson of the 'Old Buffs.'

No attack was ever made on the fort, although it was watched by large numbers of Zulus, until it was finally relieved on the 3rd April, after the garrison had been nearly six weeks on reduced rations, and after additional troops had arrived from England. The successful action of Ginginhlovo was fought by the relieving force, nearly 6,000 strong, against an army of Zulus said to have been 20,000 strong, which attacked the British entrenched camp early in the morning of the 3rd April, but was beaten off easily, with heavy loss, by rifle and artillery fire.

On this occasion also the Zulus fired off many cartridges with trifling effect, while they suffered severely from the British fire, 773 of their dead bodies being found within 1,000 yards of the entrenched camp. One battalion of the reinforcements just landed, consisting largely of raw recruits, formed part of this relieving force, which had as artillery two 9 pdr. guns, four 24pdr. rocket-tubes and two gatlings, one in each of the two divisions into which it was formed.

It will be remembered that Colonel Durnford was killed and his (2nd) Column of natives was destroyed with the 3rd Column at Isandhlwana. Colonel Evelyn Wood's 4th Column was not attacked at the same time as the columns at Isandhlwana and Inyezane, and operated afterwards in defence of Utrecht and the Transvaal. Colonel Wood established himself in an entrenched camp at Kambula Hill, and after meeting with a rather severe reverse on the 27th March, owing to a surprise due to bad outpost work, in a cattle raid at a place called Hlobane Mountain, he was heavily attacked at Kambula Hill on the 29th by a force said to be 20,000 strong, which was eventually repulsed and driven off with severe loss. The British loss on these two occasions together was about 200, of whom about 150 were killed.

The burning of Ulundi

War Mismanaged

The shocking disaster at Isandhlwana naturally caused some panic in Natal and the Transvaal; but the Zulus did not follow up their victory, and nothing occurred beyond minor raids and convoy attacks until the events at Hlobane Mountain, Kambula and Ginginhlovo at the end of March and beginning of April 1879.

By the end of April, the reinforcements which had been sent from home on the arrival of the news of Isandhlwana, had gone to the front, and Lord Chelmsford found himself in command of a force of over 22,500 of all arms, which he organised into two divisions and a flying column, the 1st Division, about 9,200 strong, under Major-General H. H. Crealock, having its headquarters at the mouth of the Tugela; the 2nd, about 10,200 strong, under Major-General Newdigate at Doornberg on the Buffalo River; and the Flying Column, about 3,100 strong, under Brigadier-General Evelyn Wood, at a new camp near the Sand Spruit, one of the sources of the white Umvolosi.

After this there was little progress made until the last days of June. On the 1st July the 2nd Division and Flying Column had arrived within 10 miles of Ketchwayo's *kraal* at Ulundi, when some futile negotiations took place and an armistice was arranged till the 3rd July. On that day after the armistice had expired, there was a reconnaissance by a considerable body of mounted troops, which nearly fell into an ambuscade and had to make a helter-skelter return to camp.

Next day, on the 4th of July, the British Army, just over 4,000 strong, with 12 guns and 1,000 natives, moved out in hollow square formation and were attacked by the Zulu Army, said to be 20.000 strong. The Zulus advanced to within 70 yards of the British square, which must have shot badly, and then gave way to the fire that was poured into them. The 17th Lancers and Irregular Horse then attacked and pursued for some distance until the enemy were dispersed or had found shelter. The Zulu casualties were estimated to be about 1,000 in killed alone. The British casualties were 12 killed and 70 wounded.

When the pursuit was over the mounted troops were sent to

Death of Zulu Warrior at Ulundi

destroy the Ulundi *kraals*, which they burnt, and, later in the day, the British Army returned to camp without making any attempt or arrangement to follow up their victory, or to capture the king. Stranger still, they commenced at once a retrograde march on Natal, Lord Chelmsford resigning his command and proceeding with a large staff direct to Pietermaritzburg. Thus was the bubble of the Zulu military power burst! The Zulus made no visible attempt at a rally, although, thanks to Lord Chelmsford's arrangements, or rather to his neglect of obviously advisable precautions, there was nothing to prevent such an attempt.

It will be remembered that the ridiculously named Flying Column on which the energy and activity of Evelyn Wood were wasted, acted with the 2nd Division in the advance on Ulundi and in the final action there.

I will now turn to the proceedings of the 1st Division, under Major-General H. H. Crealock, on whose staff I had been appointed Commanding Royal Engineer.

When the 1st Division was formed, it was 9,215 strong, of all ranks, and when Lord Chelmsford told me at Durban of my appointment to it, he said, 'You will get to Ulundi long before any of us—yours is far the easiest route.' As things turned out, the division sat at the mouth of the Tugela for about three months, then advanced some thirty miles (measured in a straight line), halted there while the action at Ulundi was fought, went back thence (without me!)—and was broken up, having lost very many valuable lives from fever, dysentery and so forth, for which the mouth of the Tugela was one of the worst places in that part of the country.

Our general's health was not good, and he suffered from various disabilities which showed up during the time he commanded us, one of the worst being a painful ailment which frequently prevented his mounting a horse for days together! He was a very accomplished amateur artist, being particularly clever at depicting horses, dogs, deer and similar subjects.

I remember that one day I was with him when he was on a horse, seeing a lot of men, white and black, bathing, and that he perpetrated a fairly good joke. You must know, good reader, that

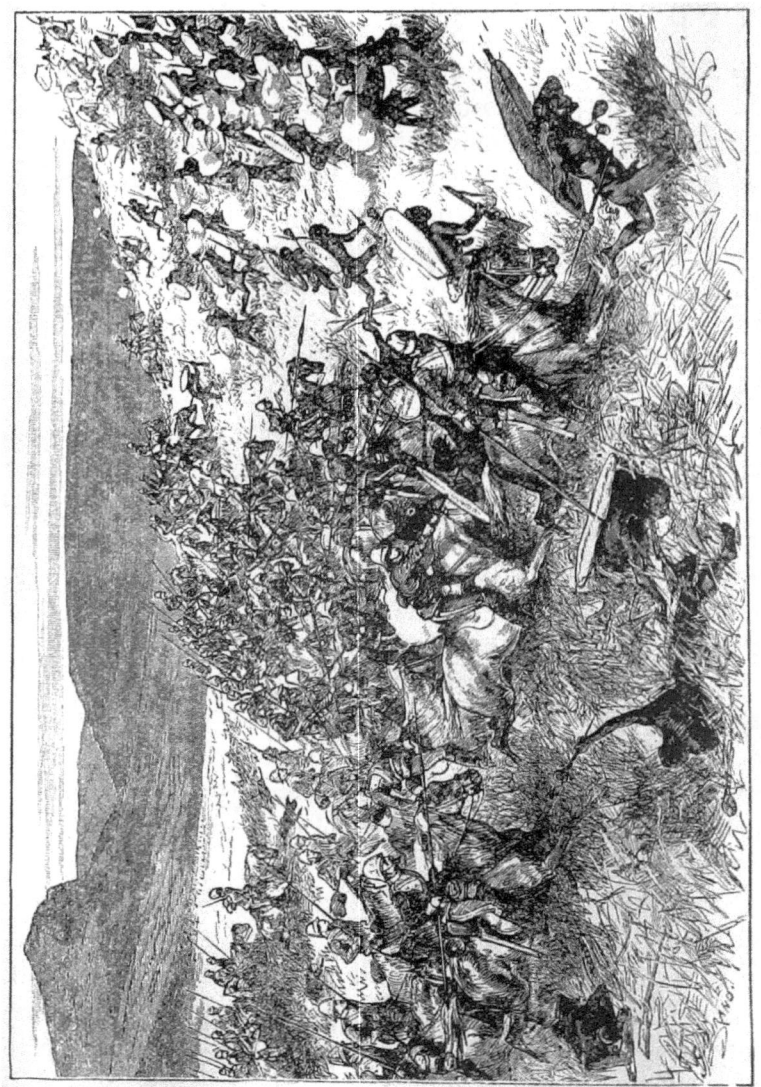

CHARGE OF THE 17TH LANCERS AT ULUNDI.

the Zulus had a great opinion of the virtues of salt water when taken internally, but as this could not be comfortably managed by the mouth, it was arranged otherwise, by the interposition of a long bullock's horn through which the water was poured. The general on seeing many operations of this sort being performed on the Zulu bathers, on all fours, exclaimed—'Behold! The Zulu horn is exalted!' He did an excellent sketch of the scene afterwards.

I remember that on this and other similar occasions I was much struck with the superiority of our men to the Zulus, and all other natives, in muscular and physical development generally.

The last time I know of white soldiers being flogged (I carefully avoided *seeing* it) was during the time we spent at the mouth of the Tugela in 1879. One Sunday in the middle of the day we of the staff were all busy in our tents, when suddenly there was a tremendous hullabaloo and a rush of men through the camp, some tumbling over tent ropes and others pulling up the pegs and throwing tents down. On looking out I saw a large party of men, madly drunk, and making the disturbance, while an increasing number of others were trying to stop it, and to seize the disturbers.

With our help and that of our soldier servants this was soon done; and we learnt that the delinquents were a party of the old 'Faugh-a-ballaghs,' wild Connaught 'boys,' who being on commissariat 'fatigue,' were rashly entrusted with the conveying of kegs of rum from one place to another. In doing this they managed to annex and hide a keg, and so got blind drunk on the contents. They all were tried by drum-head court-martial and got a couple of dozen apiece well laid on, which I have no doubt did a lot of good to them and to others like them who had to see it.

We had a most interesting man attached to our staff as a guide and adviser, and, as we should have said in India, a 'Political Officer.' His name was John Dunn and he was the son of a retired Indian Navy officer, who had finished his life in South Africa, where he had come on retirement with his wife and family. John Dunn found his way to Zululand in Panda's time, soon established a character for honesty and trustworthiness, and lived among the Zulus for many years, farming and doing a sort of agency business for them, chiefly in connection with the sale of their cattle. One constantly heard the natives say, 'Jone Doon he good man—Jone Doon he honest man.' He was a friend to Ketchwayo and I am sure did his best to prevent the war; and when it broke out, he joined us with his flocks and herds and followers, many of them ladies and children of various ages. He built a regular *kraal* a mile or so from our camp and we often went to have meals of sorts with him, when he used to give us excellent food, more or less *à la* Zulu.

In those days the Zulu young ladies before marriage wore nothing in the way of clothes only belts of woven grass or leather round their waists; after marriage they indulged in petticoats! So, one day I was at Dunn's *kraal* talking to one of his married ladies who knew some English, and remarked to her that a girl of about fifteen her daughter as it turned out was nice-looking.

So, she said, 'Yes—very good figure—you can crack a flea on her—,' not mentioning anything hard, like the thumbnail, as might have been expected! I was informed afterwards that the expression used by the lady was quite usual among the Zulus, and I must say I thought it to the point.

Another day I was riding towards Dunn's *kraal* with a large escort behind me, when we met a party of Zulu women and girls carrying milk to a depot, we had arranged for it, and among them was the young lady I have mentioned above. I had turned my escort off the road, and halted a moment to talk to the women, who were full of remarks, complimentary and otherwise, of which we understood some! Presently I noticed that the young lady had on a very smart waist-belt, and I offered to swop my sword-belt—an old gold-laced one with a silver-mounted clasp—for her belt.

To my surprise she jumped at the deal so I took off my belt (my sword was on my saddle) and gave it to her, when she slipped behind a bush, made the change, and came back with her belt in her hand ready for me.

As she had nothing on her besides the belt and some bracelets with a piece of muslin like a sash round her neck, one did not see the necessity for the retirement behind the bush however, custom ordered it, so there was no more to be said. The girl was wonderfully pleased with my belt; especially the 'slings,' swinging against her legs, seemed to delight her. I still have her belt.

Of course, the shocking affair of the death of the prince imperial was a dreadful blow to us all and to our pride in the service, I felt it specially, as I had been presented to the prince at Durban and met him frequently there, liking very much what I saw of him.

The story of the disaster is simple. On the 1st June 1879, Lieut. Carey of the 98th, attached to the Q.M.G. Department of the 1st Division of Lord Chelmsford's army, was sent out to inspect the site for a new camp, with an escort of six mounted white men of Bettington's Horse and a Kafir guide. The prince imperial obtained leave to accompany the party and went with them. At luncheon time the party halted near a village close to a small stream and off-saddled, meaning to halt for an hour. There was an open space close to the village, but high grass and crops were near and there was a deep ravine with jungle running down to the stream and forming an easy approach; and by this ravine a party of Zulus did approach, lay hid in the grass and waited for a good target.

Meanwhile the reconnoitring party acted as if they were in Hyde Park, and took their ease without any precaution whatever. Presently the Kafir guide while carrying water, put up one of the hostile ambuscades, in the grass near the stream, who bolted and disappeared. But even this did not disturb the equanimity of our reconnoitring party. They saddled up at leisure, formed up and had 'prepared to mount,' when, as they doubtless gave the target waited for, the ambuscaders fired and hit nobody. But Carey and five of his men got on their horses and galloped off helter-skelter for some miles, losing one, who was shot directly after the start, deserting him as well as another whose horse broke away, and also the Kafir guide and the prince, whose horse was awkward to mount.

The man whose horse had bolted was promptly killed, the Kafir also was surrounded and killed, while the prince's horse knocked him down and broke away, the prince being killed with *assegais*. The usual story was and is that 50 or 60 Zulus attacked the party, forty of them firing a volley at 520 yards; but I was told by John Dunn and others what was much more likely to be the truth, namely that the attackers were only nine at most in number, and that they were not all armed with fire-arms. It is inconceivable that 'a volley fired from forty rifles at a distance of twenty yards,' at eight men and eight horses close together, even if fired by Zulus, should have missed them all. (*History of the Zulu War, 1879,* by A. Wilmot: Leonaur, 2010.)

Carey and his party apparently did not fire a shot, their carbines being unloaded when they were attacked, and the two officers' revolvers being doubtless carried, as is usual with us in our army, in a manner that rendered them useless at short notice. At all events Carey and the prince appear not to have used their revolvers, with which, if they had kept their heads and could shoot, they could have easily held off the Zulus and defeated them ultimately, even if there had been a good deal more than nine of them.

Of course, I have frequently seen men lose their nerve on active service, as well as when hunting dangerous game; and an amusing instance occurred under my observation soon after Carey's case. After the 1st Division moved, towards the end of June 1879, I rode out in the afternoon one day with an escort of a couple of hundred mounted men to look at a river five or six miles ahead which we intended to bridge next day. At a short distance from camp, I came across an officer doing a sketch of the road, and he asked to be allowed to go on with me to see the road further on. So, he came and we rode on together till we came to the river, which was narrow and deep with a bluff on the other side.

There was a ford which was deep at the time, and the best place for the bridge was said to be at the bluff; so I halted and disposed my escort to cover me, and my friend and I rode on to the river with a few files scouting a little in front of me and on both flanks. We halted on the bank of the river opposite the bluff and my friend and I were making notes, when suddenly a volley was fired on the top of the bluff and there was some shouting there. We did not see anyone at first, but my friend said 'Hullo! this is a bad business,' turned his horse and galloped off to the escort. I much admired the way his horse, a nice English hunter about 15.2 high, went over the bad ground, and I thought what a good pig-sticker he might make, if one had him at Roorkee or Meerut.

However, I signalled my scouts to join me and fell back at a discreet pace, utilising the cover, and we all reached the escort safe and sound. In fact, I doubt if the Zulus on the bluff saw us until we were too far off for their limited marksmanship.

My friend always used to look unhappy afterwards when we met, although I never said a word about the occurrence to him, or anyone else, for at least fifty years.

Ending The Zulu War

At the end of May 1879, Sir Garnet Wolseley was appointed to the supreme civil and military control of the eastern part of South Africa, and he consequently arrived at Durban on the 27th June. Sometime before this a landing-place had been selected at Port Durnford, about 30 miles or so north of the Tugela, and the sappers had arranged for Sir Garnet's landing there, according to a local plan which was most simple and ingenious.

First there was a boat with a keel-less bottom, just like a spoon, decked, with a shallow well aft; rigged with one mast, shrouds and a forestay, all with slip-knotted lanyards, and a shifting lug-sail. She was also fitted with a large sheave on the stem and another on the stern-post, to take a five- or six-inch rope cable on board, under which the boat could travel ahead or astern; and an arrangement in the well for a stopper on the cable with which to control her movement.

Secondly there was a manila rope cable fixed to a bollard, above high-water mark on land, and at the other end to an anchor straight out in the sea outside the surf, with buoys at suitable places between.

When passengers or stores, or both together, had to be landed, and the surf was not too heavy, they were stowed below in the boat and battened down; the boat making sail to the cable which was picked up outside the surf. Then everything was made snug, the crew took to the rigging, except one man for the stopper, and the boat was committed to the surf, which, thanks to the skilful manipulation of the stopper, took the boat to land and bumped her into shoal water.

There the cargo was landed with the greatest ease by the smart boatmen and natives, who were used to the arrangements and were in attendance. The boat went out to sea in a similar manner, the stopper being handled so as to utilise the outdraft of the surf. All of us, sappers especially, were delighted with this beautifully simple dodge, and with the smartness of the boatmen who worked it.

But unfortunately, Sir Garnet was not able to land at Port Durnford, and had to go round by Durban and Pietermaritzburg to the front after all.

He came to Port Durnford and was battened down with his staff and baggage in the landing-boat and spent two or three hours trying to land. But although the surf had been all right up to about six o'clock that morning, it got bad afterwards, and there had been so much delay about the start that landing was too dangerous when the boat came to the surf, and so Sir Garnet had to go back to his warship. He and his staff undoubtedly had a shocking time for two hours or so while battened down in the landing-boat, in rather a rough sea, and they would not hear of trying again, but were off to Durban at once! Of course, next morning there was a flat calm, and they could have landed in rowboats if they had stayed.

A few days after this, on the 4th July 1879, the Battle of Ulundi was fought, and then the 1st Division was ordered back to be broken up and I was told to go at once to join the headquarters of my company which were with a column somewhere near Ulundi. I started off the day I got my orders, soon picked up the column I was looking for and stayed with it some days, glad to see my company again, but having a very easy time and uninteresting, except for an occurrence on one night.

On this night I was sleeping on the ground as usual under one of our carts, with two brother officers, when we were awakened by an outburst of firing which spread all over the camp. We were quickly out from under our cart, and the first thing I saw was a man rolling about and yelling in an extraordinary manner. I of course thought he must have 'stopped a bullet,' but on going up and laying hold of him I found there was nothing the matter with him except funk. So, I gave him a little encouragement with the toe of my boot, and he came to his senses, retrieved his rifle and came with me to have a look round and find his battalion.

I soon discovered that a first-class panic had occurred, no one knew how or why, that the outposts had come in, leaving arms, helmets, blankets, etc., which I saw being brought in by fatigue parties in the morning, and that an extraordinary number of men had quite lost their heads and were blazing away with ball-cartridges in all sorts of directions, but luckily in the air for the most part! I never saw such a scene, and as it was a dark night it was difficult to deal with, so that we could not stop the firing for some time.

Next day we discovered that the scare had been caused by an outpost sentry firing his rifle, having mistaken, as some people said, a cow in some bushes for a Zulu Army! We were told that no one was hurt, but we had some difficulty in believing this.

A day or two after this scare I was ordered to join Sir Garnet's Staff at Ulundi, halting one night on the way with another column, which curiously enough had a scare on the night we were with it, quite insignificant however compared with that I have described. When we arrived at Ulundi arrangements were being made to capture Ketchwayo who was still at large some 40 or 50 miles to the north. Several mounted parties were sent out, and among the rest was one under Herbert Stewart, then a major I think, consisting of fifteen officers with Kafir guides.

I was sent with this, and we had about ten days of riding long distances and roughing it. At last, we picked up Ketchwayo's tracks or rather his pony's and got within a few miles of him. I

KETCHWAYO

followed him down to a river where he had come to a quicksand and turned off half a mile or so to a ford which he had crossed the same day. As soon as I was certain about this, I halted and sent for the rest of the party, which had got scattered.

Meanwhile, before my message about the ford had reached him, Herbert Stewart had arrived at the river bank and not knowing of the quicksand, etc., had ridden in and promptly gone over his head, his horse being got out with some difficulty. This caused so much delay that we bivouacked for the night near the ford, and when we took up Ketchwayo's tracks next morning they led us straight to him in the camp of the party under Major Marter of the King's Dragoon Guards, to whom he had surrendered that morning. So, we returned to Ulundi rather sad at our bad luck!

Directly after this I was ordered with several other officers to make rapid surveys north of Ulundi, and my share of the work was the eastern portion, from the part already mapped near the sea to a line drawn north from Ulundi. The work was to last a fortnight or so, and we were to do as much as we could in that time. I started off with a party of native Pioneers under a white officer, and after a few days we found ourselves among people who had not heard of the capture of Ketchwayo and the end of the war. However, we had no trouble until one day when we saw a great many guinea-fowl near a village, and decided to halt there and have a look at the guinea-fowl after lunch.

So having arranged with the headman for beaters, we sat down to lunch and after we had finished, one of my orderlies came up and explained that the villagers had arranged to attack and kill us in the evening, so as to get our guns and pistols. After considering the matter I decided to have the shoot as arranged, and to do a little revolver practice afterwards, to show the villagers what they were in for, if they attacked us.

So, we went out and got a good bag of guinea-fowl, the villagers evidently being much impressed by our shooting; and then, the headman having asked about our revolvers which we had on us, I expended a few cartridges on different marks, showing the 'quick draw,' shooting from the hip, etc., etc., at all of which I had made myself much more proficient than Englishmen usually take the trouble to be. So, we parted the best of friends, and my orderly told us after dinner that the headman had explained to the villagers that too many of them would get shot if they attacked us, and that they had thought better of it accordingly. Of course, we took precautions just the same, but nothing happened and we departed in peace next day.

An interesting Zulu custom came to light in some of the more out-of-the-way villages. This was that whenever specially eligible-looking travellers came to them, they sought to improve the breed in the villages by arranging for the production of children by the visitors. In this connection overtures were frequently made to my Pioneer friend and to me, as we were evidently thought highly likely individuals. I had come across similar ways in India, among Hindus in the Himalayas, and among some of the more primitive of the Afghan and frontier Muhammadans in the early days of my service in the East.

During this surveying trip I came across many specimens of the honey bird. This is a little fowl about the size and appearance of a sparrow, that one sees, especially in the morning as one rides along in the jungle. It goes fluttering about from one bush to another chirruping to attract attention, and if you follow, it leads you straight to a bees' nest, which your Kafirs proceed to rob, taking away the honey for breakfast and leaving the comb containing young bees stuck on thorns for the honey bird to eat. Thanks to these little birds we had quite good honey at breakfast nearly every morning.

I also frequently heard lions and leopards at night, and saw their tracks by day, but we never saw any of these animals themselves. We managed to shoot a good number of guinea-fowl, florican of sorts, partridges and quail, also some plover, snipe and ducks, so that we did not fare badly with the help of sweet potatoes, Indian corn, etc., etc., that we bought from the villagers.

One of my stations was a high bluff at the junction of two rivers where there was a deep pool with a good many crocodiles in it. We were told that this was named the 'Cliff of the Vultures' and was one of the places of execution used by Chaka and Dingaan about fifty to sixty years before. It was said that sometimes the bodies were too many for the crocodiles, or caught as they fell down the bluff, when the vultures had their turn.

In due time we got back to Ulundi with quite a successful sketch, when my captain of Pioneers, to whom I had taken a liking, did not appear for three days having 'got drunk every day,' as my orderly 'Adona' told me; apparently regarding that proceeding as a matter of course!

At Ulundi I found the headquarters of my company and rejoined them, marching off with them directly afterwards *via* Etshowe and the Tugela mouth, to Pinetown, nine or ten miles inland from Durban, for final orders.

I had a very pleasant and interesting time at Ulundi before and after I went surveying, as Sir Garnet Wolseley sent for me to ride with him and talk about India almost every evening. He was very well read and well educated both as a soldier and otherwise, and he had had much war experience, and since I also was not unqualified in the former respects, I could and did appreciate, enjoy and profit by his conversation. He was a man of very high ideals of duty and of loyalty, and I came to regard him with respect, admiration and strong personal liking. I have always felt that England did not have her usual luck with Lord Wolseley, in that he did not synchronise with the Boer War and the Great War.

I only remember one amusing incident on the march to Pinetown. We halted at the Tugela mouth for a couple of days, and I was taking a stroll with one of my subalterns one evening when we stopped and sat down to see a kit inspection, a little way off, of a squadron of Bettington's Horse. Colonel Bettington rode up and proceeded with the inspection, in the course of which he knocked down two of his troopers quite neatly. I was told that they were all in great awe of him. I met him that evening at dinner with the *commandant* of the post, that best of good fellows whom his friends called Reggie Thynne. Bettington was medium sized, very strong, a fine horseman, good-looking and a good fellow, in fact a first-class fighting man, as he had learnt to be handy with his weapons from long experience in South

American Republics. I had a very pleasant talk with him and wished I had met him sooner. I was very sorry to see an announcement of his death from fever in South America, two or three years later.

At Pinetown we found the King's Dragoon Guards and 17th Lancers both literally very much out at elbows and armpits as they had been soldiering in their tunics, I think the last corps in our army that did so on active service. But if they were out at elbows they were not out of spirits, and we all amused ourselves in various ways. I remember that we had quite good fun paper-chasing, as we could ride over the country in September without doing damage, and the neighbouring farmers were most kind and good-natured to us.

I paid a visit to Pietermaritzburg, the capital of Natal, directly after I arrived at Pinetown, travelling by post-cart drawn by capital four-horse teams most of the way but with an extra pair and a postilion for a long hill, called I think Inkantla Hill, when we went up. One morning at Pietermaritzburg I met one of the Pioneers who had been with me surveying in Zululand, and he explained that he was in attendance on the law courts, giving evidence about the captain who had also been with me, now in jail, and being tried for embezzling some of the men's pay.

Before I went back to Pinetown my company was ordered upcountry, and I had instructions to embark at once for home, *en route* to Kabul, where fighting was going on, and where a place was waiting for me. So, I hurried back to Pinetown and embarked at Durban on the next mail steamer for home.

The ship was lying in the open sea, the harbour of Durban being too shallow then for large vessels, as ships of 3,000 tons or so were considered in those days, and I went on board in a tender, after bidding *adieu* to many friends and last of all to my faithful Zulu orderly Adona, or Adonis as of course we called him. The last I remember of him was seeing him sitting weeping on the shore, in an old suit of khaki uniform I had given him. He sat there for an hour or more, and after that he disappeared. He was a good fellow and feared nothing except ghosts!

The ship rolled deeply as there was a long swell, and to my

astonishment I was sea-sick for a couple of hours after I got on board. However, I was all right after a little sleep, and soon discovered that two of the male passengers were soldiers and old friends. Of course, we arranged to sit together, and having chosen a table in a retired corner, we were (at first unpleasantly) surprised at dinner-time to find a lady, who turned out to be an American actress, and her *duenna* established at our table. I am quite certain that no-one of us showed the least trace of surprise or disappointment especially as the lady was good looking. But she at once apologised for invading our table, saying, 'You see I couldn't sit with those cats'! and was otherwise pleasant and amusing, so we thought ourselves very lucky long before dinner was over, and still more so later on.

We stopped at East London next day and I saw a leper, a half caste Hottentot, taken on board. He travelled in a big packing-box which was half-filled with straw and carried in an uncovered boat hung to davits at the side of the ship. A number of holes had been bored in the lid of the box, which was shut down at night, an awning being arranged to keep out rain. We changed at Port Elizabeth into the newest of the mail-steamers, of 3,200 tons, in which we averaged 13 knots from Cape Town to Madeira—a speed thought wonderful at that time!

We were a couple of days at Cape Town, which I spent pleasantly with gunner friends in the barracks, and so went on board again. As we were starting, I saw an acquaintance, a tall good-looking fellow with a red head, who had served with us as a volunteer, bidding *adieu* to a lady on the quay. The lady was tearful and very sad, and Red-head was doing his best to console her. But of course, parting was inevitable, and he came on board at last looking most melancholy.

Two or three days afterwards our American actress—who was thoroughly established in the good graces of myself and two friends, in fact three, as an excellent Royal Navy sailor had been discovered and roped in—begged of me to walk with her regularly to save her from my red-headed friend, who, as she put it, 'had become a nuisance'! In other words, he had been hopelessly 'smitten' by her! After what I had seen on the quay at Cape

Town, I felt quite shocked, and all the more readily did as I was invited, having to stand a little chaff in consequence.

Then I had a further shock to my finer feelings from being told that Red-head was a married man with a family! And finally, our American friend told me that he had seriously asked her to run away with him when they reached England! She said he 'claimed' to be very rich, and made all sorts of promises—but she seemed to have got rid of him somehow.

When we were off Cape Verde, our engines broke down—a quite common event in those days—and as it was a dead calm, we lay rolling about surrounded by a couple of hundred sharks, nearly all small, six or eight feet long; but there were two or three monsters. One that I saw, of the hammer-headed variety, must have been at least 18 feet long. He kept about a hundred yards from the ship, but the smaller ones crowded round and ate any odds and ends we threw to them. We tried to catch one, but there were no proper hooks or tackle on the ship, so we were not successful.

We ran into the heaviest gale I ever was in at sea, when we approached Madeira, and could not land there in consequence. The hatchways were all battened down, and the seas were tremendous. We passed a very pretty brig hove to, and when we looked down at her from the top of a big wave, while she was at the bottom of the next hollow, the effect was fine. I remember that she was making excellent weather of it, under fore-and-aft sails with everything else snug. We kept on running before the wind, and it was most interesting to watch the seas coming up aft of us—each one looking as if it must come on board, though none did.

We arrived in Southampton Docks at a late hour one evening, and I learned that I had been promoted to brevet-major for my services in Zululand. The country was under about six inches of snow, and the temperature was considerably changed from what it was nine days before, when we crossed the Line! Directly we stopped and a tender came alongside, we saw our red-headed friend hurrying with a bag in his hand, of course as we thought, in haste to greet his wife and family. But next morning when we landed and the American lady and I happened to go to breakfast together after passing our baggage, we saw our friend with a remarkably good-looking and well-turned-out lady, whose name in the registration book, we were shocked to find, was quite different from his.

I went on to London, and when I reported myself, found orders waiting for me to proceed *via* Brindisi to join Sir Frederick Roberts' command at Kabul; and after I had got some clothes together I proceeded accordingly.

The Services of Royal Engineers During the Zulu War, 1879

(An extract from *The History of the Royal Engineers* by Whitworth Porter)

The development of our possessions in South Africa was from this time continuous, and culminated in the annexation of the Transvaal in 1878. In consequence of this transaction, we became involved in difficulties with the Zulus, which led to the disastrous war of 1879, many of the details of which are of much interest to the Engineer.

It having been decided that an advance should be made into Zululand for the attack of Ketchwayo and the capture of Ulundi, two field companies of the Engineers (the 2nd and the 5th) embarked for South Africa on December 2nd, 1878, and landed at Durban on January 4th, 1879, for the reinforcement of the corps in South Africa. This had previously only consisted of the 7th Company, commanded by Major F.W. Nixon, who had under him Lieutenants F. H. MacDowel and J. Clarke.

Colonel A.W. Durnford, assisted by Captain A. H. Hine, who was at the time Colonial Engineer, had organised and equipped three Companies of Native Pioneers. These each consisted of 1 captain and 2 subalterns (European), and 4 sergeants and 96 sappers (native). In each company twenty-five men were armed with the Martini-Henry rifle, the remainder bearing *assegais* and shields. Each man also carried a tool slung. The equipment of tools, forges, dynamite, &c., was loaded in two-wheeled oxcarts.

The officers were gentlemen employed in the Colonial Engineers department, when the expeditionary force was organised. Colonel Durnford took command of the entire Natal Native Contingent, consisting of three battalions of 1,000 men each, with 450 mounted men and a rocket battery under Captain Russell, R.A. From long residence in the colony and from having commanded similar contingents during previous outbreaks. Colonel Durnford had acquired great influence over the natives of Natal and Basutoland, and it was felt that no one else was so well qualified to handle this auxiliary force.

Colonel Hassard was Commanding Royal Engineer, and Lieutenant J. C. Baxter was adjutant. The other officers and Companies were divided amongst the three columns which were intended to penetrate into the district from different points.

Colonel E. Wood commanded that which was to start from Utrecht; with him was Major Moysey. Colonel Glyn's column was to start from Helpmakaar and Rorke's Drift; with him was the 5th Field Company Royal Engineers, with Captain W. P. Jones, Lieutenants R. M. Chard, R. Da C. Porter, and C. E. Commeline, also two Companies of Native Pioneers commanded by Lieutenant F. H. Macdowel.

A third column, under Colonel Pearson, was to cross the Tugela River near its mouth. With him was the 2nd Field Company, with Captain W. R. C. Wynne, Lieutenants D. C. Courtney, H. B. Willock, and C. E. Haynes; also, one Company of Native Pioneers under lieutenant T. R. Main.

Lieutenants V. J. Yorke and Brice were appointed Assistant Engineers, and took charge of the bridge equipment for crossing the Tudela. Lieutenant-General Lord Chelmsford was in command of the combined force.

The main Engineer interest in the campaign centres in the catastrophe of Isandlwana and the defence of Rorke's Drift, in the former of which Colonel A. Durnford met his glorious death, and at the latter Lieutenant Chard made an equally glorious and at the same time successful resistance to an attack by overwhelming numbers of Zulus. The column under Colonel

Glyn, which the lieutenant-general commanding accompanied, crossed the Buffalo River at Rorke's Drift on January 20th, advanced as far as Isandlwana and there encamped.

On the same day Colonel Durnford arrived at Rorke's Drift with five troops of the Mounted Natives, Russell's rocket battery, and two companies of the contingent infantry. On the morning of the 22nd he received an order from Lord Chelmsford to move up to Isandlwana camp with his mounted men and rocket battery. He started for that point at about 8 a.m. and reached his destination at 11 a.m. There he found that a number of Zulus had been seen on the top of the adjacent hills, and that an attack was expected.

The troops at Isandlwana at the time consisted of six companies of the 24th Regiment, two guns of Royal Artillery, and a few mounted men. The remainder of the column had moved on with Lord Chelmsford some miles to the front, with the object of attacking a Zulu *impi* supposed to be collected in the vicinity.

The mounted men of Lonsdale's Native Contingent were on outpost duty as scouts, and messages were constantly being received from them:—"The enemy are in force behind the hills to the left;" "The enemy are in three columns;" "The columns are separating, one moving to the left rear and one towards the general."

Durnford now decided on quitting the camp with his mounted men, and endeavouring to prevent the column referred to from joining the *impi* which it was imagined was at the time engaged with the troops under Lord Chelmsford. He sent two troops of the Mounted Natives on to the hills at the left, to ascertain more clearly the enemy's movements, and he himself with the remaining two troops, and Russell's rocket battery escorted by a company of the Native Contingent, moved to the front.

Having proceeded some distance he received a report that an immense *impi* was behind the hills to his left, and almost immediately afterwards the Zulus appeared in great strength in his front, and on the left. They were in skirmishing order, but

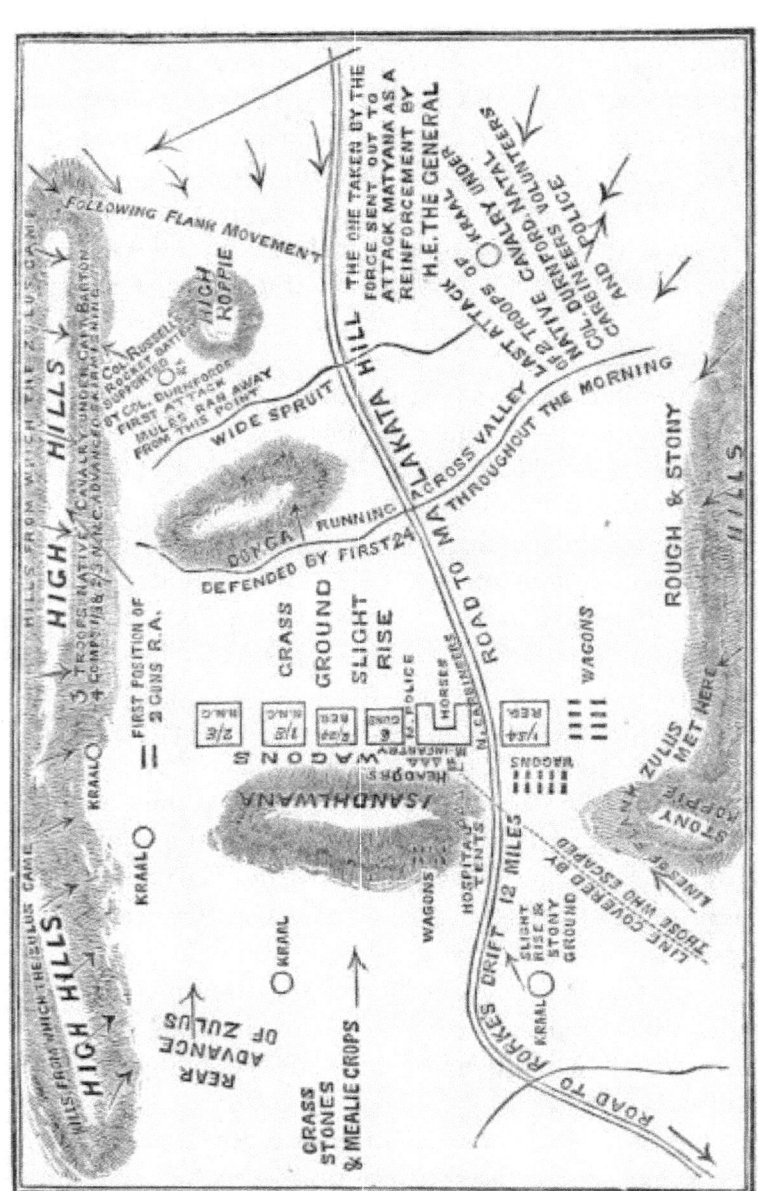

SKETCH OF THE BATTLE OF ISANDHLWANA.

ten or twelve deep, with supports close behind. They advanced with extreme rapidity, and opened fire when about 800 yards distant. Durnford retired slowly until he reached a *donga* or watercourse, where he took up a position. Finding the strength of the enemy too great for him to hold this point, he resumed his retreat, keeping his men in skirmishing order, and maintaining a steady fire.

The rocket battery had not been able to advance as rapidly as Durnford with his two troops had done. They, hearing heavy firing on their left, and learning that the enemy were in that quarter, changed direction to their left. Before reaching the crest of the hills they were attacked on all sides. Only one rocket was fired, and then the Zulus were on them; the first volley dispersed the natives and mules of the troop, leaving the remainder to maintain a hand-to-hand combat, in which Captain Russell was killed. Durnford, in his retreat, came upon the remains of the rocket battery, and for a time drove the Zulus back. The whole body continued to retire as steadily as they could towards the camp, until they reached a second *donga* not very far in front of the main position.

Here a desperate stand was made, but by this time the Zulus had turned the whole position, and were in the midst of the 24th. All further cohesion was lost. Those who survived had commenced a headlong rush on the road leading back to the Buffalo River, and a great number of Durnford's men joined in the flight. He succeeded in rallying a few of the bravest and most determined of his levy, and stood firm in the position he occupied. He saw at a glance that the only chance for the fugitives was to detain the Zulus as long as possible, and resolved by the sacrifice of his life to hold the point to the last. He could easily have escaped had he chosen, for he was well mounted; but, had he done so, the lives of all on foot must have been lost.

He and those he was able to gather round him died where they stood, and thereby set an example of noble self-devotion, which was not long in bearing fruit. It was only in the succeeding year Henn followed in his footsteps, and in a precisely similar manner under the same circumstances, at the disaster of Maiwand, gave up his life to save those of his flying comrades. Well may the corps be proud of these two heroes, and love to commemorate the incidents of their heroic stand. They are, it is fondly hoped, only *primi inter pares*; and, should occasion again call for it, the Engineers will not be wanting in the supply of men capable and willing to follow these glorious examples. Meanwhile the names of Durnford and Henn stand out in the foremost rank of those who have scorned to seek safety in flight, and have known how to die with their faces to the foe.

In this fatal field, in addition to Colonel Durnford, Lieutenant MacDowel lost his life, as did also four non-commissioned officers and sappers of the 5th Company, who had been brought up to Isandlwana, on the very morning.

We must now turn to the incidents by which Lieutenant Chard's name has become connected with the memorable defence of Rorke's Drift. He was with the 5th Company, under Captain Jones, marching up the country from Durban towards Helpmakaar, when an order arrived from Lord Chelmsford, that an officer and four sappers were to be pushed forward as rapidly as possible, in order to join the column, then about to enter Zululand from Rorke's Drift. Chard, being the senior subaltern, elected to proceed in charge of the detachment, who were placed on light carts, and arrived at Rorke's Drift on January 21st.

He proceeded with his men early on the 22nd to Isandlwana, where he found that Lord Chelmsford had marched out with the larger part of the force, but had left orders that the sappers should remain in the camp, and that Chard should be stationed at Rorke's Drift, to fortify and maintain the post covering the crossing of the river, which was effected by means of ponts or ferries.

He left his men as ordered (who all lost their lives in the disaster), and on the road back met Durnford on his march to the front. He informed that officer that the Zulus appeared to be threatening the camp, and was requested to convey a message to Captain Russell, who was about a mile in rear, to hurry up with his rocket battery. This he did, and then returned to the drift, where he was placed in command of the small party at the station, by Major Spalding, who was leaving for Helpmakaar.

In his report of what followed, he says:—

> At 3.15 p.m. that day, I was watching at the ponts, when two men came towards us from Zululand at a gallop. They shouted out and were taken across the river, and I was then informed by one of them—Lieut. Adendorff, of Commandant Lonsdale's regiment, who afterwards remained to assist in the defence, of the disaster befallen at the Isandula Camp, and that the Zulus were advancing upon Rorke's Drift.
>
> I gave instructions to strike tents, and to put all stores into the wagons, while I instantly made my way to the commissariat store, and there found that a note had been received from the third column stating that the enemy was advancing in force against our post, which we were to strengthen and hold at all costs.

A company of the 24th Regiment, under Lieutenant Bromhead, was at the station, together with some details and detached men.

The following were also present:—Surgeon Reynolds, Acting-Commissary Officer Dalton, Assistant-Commissary Dunne, Mr. Byrne, Commissariat Department, Lieutenant Adendorff, of Lonsdale's regiment, and the Rev. G. Smith, with 131 non-commissioned officers and men. This formed the entire garrison. There had also been present a detachment of the Natal Native Contingent, under Captain Stephenson, but both officer and men left the post and made their way to Helpmakaar. After this desertion. Chard writes—

> I saw that our line of defence was too extended for the small number of men now left, and at once commenced an inner entrenchment of biscuit boxes, out of which we had soon completed a wall two boxes high.

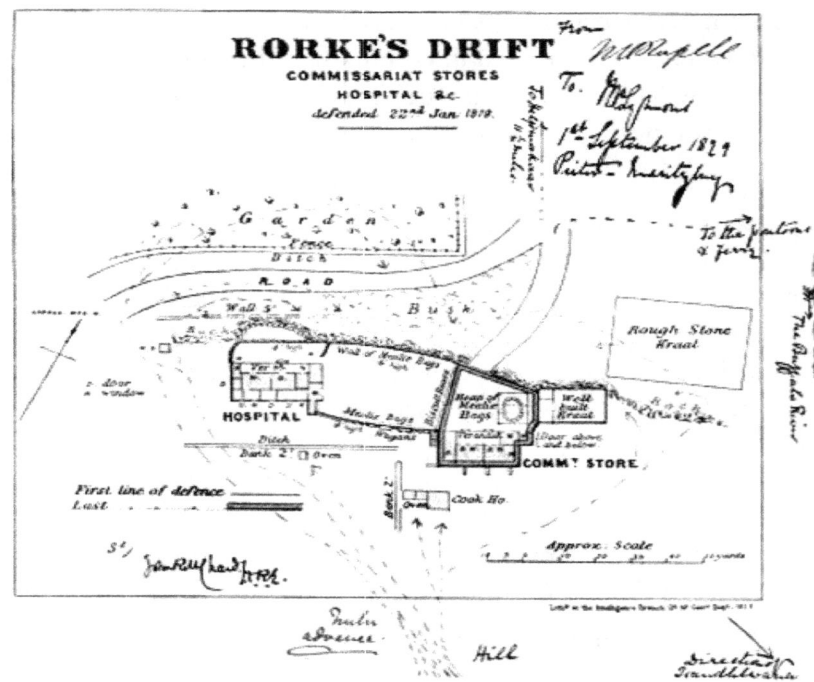

ORIGINAL SKETCH SIGNED BY CHARD

The post of Rorke's Drift was thus composed. There were two buildings, the store and the hospital, standing about 50 yards apart, running east and west, the store being to the east and projecting beyond the alignment of the hospital, thus flanking it. The inner side of the store was connected with the outer face of the hospital by a wall of mealie bags, with two wagons in the centre. Another of similar construction ran from the far corner of the inner face of the hospital, enclosing a considerable space and terminating at the further extremity of the store, where stood a well-built *kraal*, which was embraced in the general scheme of defence.

The wall of biscuit boxes built by Chard to reduce the extent of the space to be defended ran from the corner of the store nearest the hospital, to meet the wall last described, and, as events proved, was the means of securing the defence after that building was captured. The tale may be taken up in Chard's own words:—

About 4.20 p.m. five or six hundred of the enemy came suddenly in sight around the hill to the south. They advanced at a run against our south wall, but were met by a well-sustained fire; yet, notwithstanding heavy loss, they continued to advance till within fifty yards of the wall, when their leading men encountered such a hot fire from our front, with a cross one from the store, that they were checked. Taking advantage, however, of the cover afforded by the cook-house and the ovens (these were detached buildings to the south of the post), they kept up thence heavy musketry volleys; the greater number, however, without stopping at all moved on towards their left, round our hospital and thence made a rush upon the northwest wall and our breastwork of mealie bags.

After a short but desperate struggle these assailants were driven back with heavy loss into the bush around our works Another body advancing somewhat more to the left than those who first attacked us occupied a garden in the hollow of the road, and also the bush beyond it in great force, taking special advantage of the bush which, we had not had time to cut down. The enemy was thus able to advance close to our works, and in this part soon held one whole side of wall, while we on the other kept back a series of desperate assaults, which were made on a line extending from the hospital all along the wall as far as the bush

All this time the enemy had been attempting to force the hospital, and shortly afterwards did set fire to the roof. The garrison of the hospital defended the place room by room, our men bringing out all the sick who could be moved before they retired. Private Williams, Hook, R. Jones and W. Jones of the 24th Regiment were the last four men to leave, holding the doorway against the Zulus with bayonets, their ammunition being quite expended . . . . Seeing the hospital burning and desperate attempts being made by the enemy to fire the roof of our stores, we now converted two mealie bag heaps into a sort of redoubt, which gave a second line of fire all along, Assistant-Commissary Dunne working hard at this, though much exposed, thus rendering most valuable assistance.

Darkness then came on. We were completely surrounded, and after several furious attempts had been gallantly repulsed we were eventually forced to retire to the middle and then to the inner wall of our *kraal* (this *kraal* was divided into two unequal rectangles by a division wall) on the east of the position we first had. We were sustaining throughout all this a desultory fire kept up all night, and several assaults were attempted but always repulsed with vigour, the attacks continuing till after midnight, our men firing with the greatest coolness, not wasting a single shot. The light afforded by the burning hospital proved a great advantage. At four a.m. on the 23rd January firing ceased, and at daybreak the enemy were passing out of sight, over the hill to the south-west.

Such is the succinct account of this memorable defence, as given by the chief actor therein. It requires no amplification or picturesque development to add to its impressiveness. As was well said of it by the *Cape Argus:*—

> The despatch is written by a simple subaltern of Engineers, and is couched in the plainest terms; but it reads with an eloquence words alone could not give, and tells a story that will go down to posterity among the glorious traditions of the heroes of the British race . . . . Any man may be a hero in the sense of doing a brave thing in a moment; but the highest degree of heroism requires several qualities besides physical courage. Fortitude in the face of apparently overwhelming difficulties, strict obedience to duty, the calm courage that accepts labour, when necessary, as equal to fighting, endurance under seemingly crushing odds, these and other qualities were displayed at Rorke's Drift by Lieut. Chard and his companions.

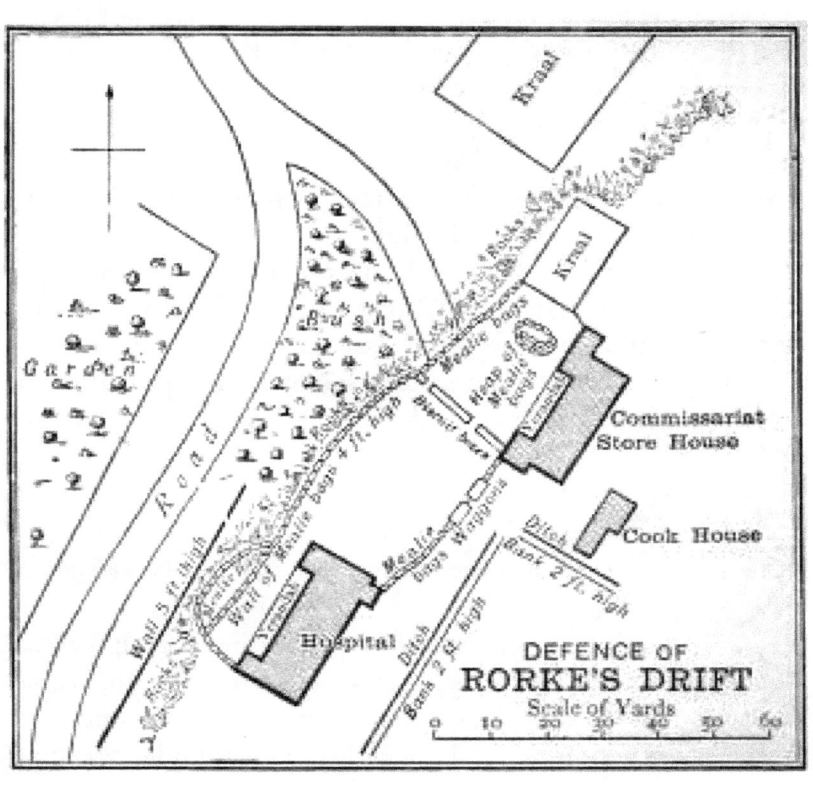

It remains only to give the statistics of numbers and casualties. We have said that there were, all told, 131 non-commissioned officers and men present; but it must be remembered that of these thirty-five were sick in hospital, very few of whom were capable of assisting in the defence. The Zulus numbered about 3,000, and left behind them 350 dead. Their wounded were removed by them when they retired. Of the little garrison seventeen were killed and ten wounded.

It is no exaggeration to say that but for this heroic and successful defence, not only would the remainder of the third column, which had escaped the disaster of Isandlwana, have been cut off, but the torrent of Zulu invasion would have poured into Natal with results that are frightful to contemplate. Lieutenant Chard was promoted "to be Captain Supernumerary to the Establishment in recognition of his gallant services in the defence of Rorke's Drift Post against the attack of the Zulus," and in the same *Gazette* he was made a brevet major. He also received the Victoria Cross.

The disastrous commencement of the campaign seriously jeopardised the safety of the column under Colonel Pearson, which, having crossed at the mouth of the Tugela, had advanced northward as far as Ekowe.

Before leaving Natal, a work had been thrown up on that side of the river called Fort Pearson; and, as soon as the Tugela had been passed, Wynne and his company of sappers were employed in the construction of another on the Zululand side, which received the name of Fort Tenedos. On January 18th the column started on their march, and, after a sharp fight at Inyezane on the 22nd, reached Ekowe on the following day. This had been a Norwegian Mission station, and was abandoned on account of the war. It consisted of a church and three other buildings, all of sundried brick. The church had a corrugated iron roof; the other houses were thatched. This point was selected as a depot for stores, and was to be fortified accordingly. Work had been begun with that object when, on the 26th, news arrived of the defeat of No. 3 Column, but without any trustworthy details.

On the 28th Wynne in his diary recorded:—

> At 10 a.m. telegram received from General Lord Chelmsford, hinting at the occurrence of a disaster, and stating that he had found it necessary to retire to the frontier; that all former plans had been given up; that Colonel Pearson must expect the Zulu force to bear down upon his column, and leaving him full discretion to retire upon the Tugela or hold his position. At a meeting of commanding officers, to which I was called, I found it had been pretty well determined to retreat at once, leaving all standing. The fort being in a tolerably advanced state, I could not concur in this decision, looking upon such a retreat as hazardous in itself, and the moral effect of it to be greatly deprecated.
> I therefore was in favour of remaining and strengthening our position to the utmost. It was, however, a question of provisions and ammunition; and about the sufficiency of these, for holding out for any length of time, there was some uncertainty. At this point Col. Walker, A.A.G., and Capt. Macgregor, A.Q.M.G., came in, and, being decidedly of the same opinion as myself, the question was again opened, and, after a short discussion, it was determined to remain, sending back to the Tugela the mounted troops.

Fortunately, on that same evening a convoy of provisions arrived in seventy-two wagons, with three companies of the 99th and two companies of the Buffs.

The decision to hold the fort having been arrived at, every effort was used to render it secure. Wynne's diary is full of detail of the labour expended by the troops, under the superintendence of his brother officers and himself, assisted by the non-commissioned officers and sappers of his company, until at length Fort Ekowe became a really formidable work. One point of interest remains to be related in connection with it.

The garrison being cooped up within the space occupied by their lines, and the whole of the country between Ekowe and the Tugela being in the hands of the Zulus, communication with the rear was completely cut off. Under these circumstances Lieutenant C Haynes, R.E., who was at the base on the Tugela, suggested the possibility of flashing simals to the beleaguered force. His idea was somewhat scouted by the authorities, still he was permitted to make the effort. The difficulty lay in the improbability of attracting the attention of those within the fort.

When all was ready, signalling was begun, and was continued with patience day by day whenever a gleam of sunshine was available. For a whole week no indication was obtained that the flashes were observed, and it was not till long after a less persevering man would have abandoned the trial that the first answering gleam was obtained. It was an unpleasant and anxious task watching on an exposed hill-top for so long, but the reward of success was great, and Haynes had the gratification of receiving the personal thanks of Lord Chelmsford for his ingenuity and patience. We find the following entries in Wynne's diary on the subject:—

> *Sunday, March 2nd*. Heliograph signals observed in the direction of the Tugela at about 3 p.m. No message made out. Endeavoured to flash sun's rays back.
>
> *March 3rd.* Today the signalling from the Tugela was again observed, and some words deciphered of which the import, though vague, seemed to be that a convoy was to be expected on the 13th inst. with 1,000 men, and that when aware of its approach Colonel Pearson was to sally out with the surplus of the garrison. This, of course, caused much excitement and canvassing of the real purport of the message, and many were the endeavours to flash something back with hand mirrors, &c. I determined to try and effect communication by means of a large screen raised above the ground, revolving on horizontal pivots, which, being brought alternately to a horizontal and vertical position in front of the place to be signalled to, should produce dashes and dots through the spaces of time of its

appearances.

Wynne had much trouble with his apparatus before he got it into working order, owing to the damage caused by tempestuous weather. At length on March 10th is the entry:—

> We signalled two or three messages to the Tugela signalling station. Signalling from thence was kept up for two or three hours.

On the following day he made his last entry in his diary, which leaves off in the middle of a sentence:—

> Had an attack of diarrhoea during the night; weak in the morning. Started at 7.30 a.m. with——

His sickness increased very rapidly, and on the relief of Ekowe on April 4th, he was moved in a cart to the Tugela River; but the frightful jolting over the rough roads proved too much for him, and he died near Fort Pearson on April 9th, 1879. Colonel Pearson, in his despatch of that day, written before he knew of Wynne's death, says:—

> The Royal Engineers, of course, took a very prominent part in the construction of Fort Ekowe. Captain Wynne's illness is much to be deplored. I consider him a most valuable officer, and his illness is entirely due to over-exertion at a time when he was in very indifferent health.

It has already been stated that Major Moysey was attached to Colonel Wood's column. At the outbreak of the war, he was at Pretoria, but he joined Wood at Utrecht with one sergeant and eleven sappers of the 7th Company. It is not necessary to trace the movements of this column with any detail, the Engineer force with it being so small. Moysey designed and carried out the construction of Fort Kambula, but he was not present when it was attacked on March 29th, having been sent back a few days before to superintend the strengthening of Fort Amiel, and he did not return to Kambula till April 1st. Consequently, only Sergeant R. Wood and ten of the sappers were in action on that day.

When the news of the check which had been received by Lord Chelmsford's forces arrived in England, immediate steps were taken to hurry out reinforcements sufficiently numerous to admit of an active renewal of the war. The Engineers were strengthened by the 30th Field Company under Lieutenant-Colonel Harrison, with Captain Blood, Lieutenants Watkins, Sherrard, MacKean, and Littledale; the right half of the C, or Telegraph Troop, under Major Hamilton, Lieutenants Hare, MacGregor, Rich, and Bond. The following officers were also sent out:—Lieutenant-Colonel Steward, as Commanding Royal Engineer to the force, Lieutenant-Colonels Webber and Hale, Captains Anstey, Heneage, Lieutenants James, Cameron, Penrose, and Brotherton.

When Lord Chelmsford decided on making his forward movement on Ulundi, after the arrival of his reinforcements, he formed a flying column under Colonel Wood, and a division (called the 2nd) under his own command. The flying column, with Moysey attached, left Kambula on May 30th, and was shortly after joined by the 5th Company Royal Engineers under Captain Jones. The 2nd Company was posted at first to Lord Chelmsford's division, but this was also eventually sent to Wood's force, it being considered advisable to have as many Engineers as possible with the troops in front.

Lieutenant Porter, of the 5th Company, wrote a diary of the march on Ulundi, from which the following extracts are taken:—

> *Monday, June 16th.* Wood crossed over to our side of the river today, and encamped just below the forts. We joined his *laager* in the afternoon.
>
> *June 18th.* Reveille at 4 a.m., started at 6.15 a.m.; marched only 5 miles. Had two difficult drifts to make, hence the short march. . . . In the afternoon we commenced a fort where a new depot is to be formed. . . .
>
> *June 21st.* Started half-an-hour later than usual, as the enemy was reported to be in sight. . . . We had a very steep hill to ascend, then a very steep descent. At the bottom we

had to cross three baddish *dongas,* and a little further on we had to cross the river. All this necessitated a good deal of work, and though we only went about 5 miles, we did not get in very early....

June 22nd. The road proved very difficult, and we only did three miles. First, we had to ascend a very steep hill, the wagons forming *laager,* and outspanning as they came up. In the meantime, the company was at work about 1½ mile further on, blasting a passage through a rocky cliff.... A big *laager* was formed at the foot of the hill. About half a mile further on, on a neck connecting the hill we had descended with another which we shall have to climb when we move on, was a small *laager* in which we (the 2nd Company, as well as ours, for that has now joined the flying column) and the 13th are encamped. We commenced a new fort here, to be called Fort Evelyn. It is built chiefly of sods, with a small ditch outside, and is a pentagon without any flanking arrangements. Command 6' ditch 8', to be increased as time may permit.

June 24th. Marched at 6.30 a.m. Road again very difficult. It wound about like a snake, up and down steep hills, so that progress was very slow, and drag ropes in constant use. ... From the hills Ulundi can be seen, apparently about 20 miles off as the crow flies.

Similar entries occur until Ulundi was nearly reached.

July 2nd. Commenced building a small pentagonal stone fort. The ideas for the future are these. Tomorrow or next day the army is to cross the Umvalosi, without wagons, except such as are necessary for ammunition and tools. The men are to carry two days' provisions. The wagons are to be left behind in *laager,* one battalion guarding them. All day long we could see large numbers of Zulus in the big *kraals* across the river. Some of them have been dancing war dances.

July 4th. Started in the dark to cross the river.... The river was about 50 yards wide, nowhere more than eighteen inches deep; the bottom sandy. After crossing, we commenced at once to ascend through a somewhat broken country towards the open plains where the *kraals* lay... About 2 miles from the river, we got into open grass land, and here we formed a large square two deep. The Engineers (only the 5th Company, as the 2nd Company had been left on the other side of the river with the force guarding the *laager*) were in reserve on the front face, behind the Gatlings. About 8 o'clock large bodies of the enemy began to appear, both to the right and left of us, and soon after on our front also. We did not see any in our rear, but we heard afterwards from the garrison left behind in the *laager*, that a very large force, estimated at about 10,000 men, had passed down the valley of the river shortly after we had crossed.

It appears from the account of prisoners taken during the battle, that the Zulus intended to attack the camp that morning. For this purpose, a large body was sent down the river; this afterwards came up on our rear. The two other bodies began working through the hills on each flank, and had we not advanced ourselves, a concentric attack would have been made. As it was, we came out into the open, to the vast astonishment of the Zulus, who thought we were moonstruck and delivered into their hands. They accordingly made arrangements to surround us on the line of march. The people on the two flanks turned about and came abreast of us at a distance of a mile and a half, while the body originally intended to act as a reserve now attacked our front face.

Altogether there were about 20,000 of the enemy present, but only about half of that number ever got close to us. At 8.50 a.m. our cavalry on the front and flanks became engaged, and about ten minutes after they had to retire on the main body and get inside the square. About this time the first bullets began to whistle about our heads. By 9.5 a.m. all four faces were attacked, and a heavy fire opened by both sides. About 9.25 a.m. the pressure on the left of the left face began to be rather great, and our company was moved there in support. At 9.35 a.m. the Zulus retired, and a few minutes afterwards the cavalry was sent out to follow them up.... Notwithstanding the somewhat heavy fire to which my company was exposed, we had only a sergeant wounded, and this seemed the more surprising, as a good many bullets struck the ground among us. The N. N. Pioneers next to us had 2 officers and 3 men hit, whilst the N. I. behind us had 7 men hit.... About 11 o'clock the cavalry set fire to Ulundi, and the army was marched towards the *kraal* to see the burning.

The Engineers within the square during the battle were—Colonel Harrison, A.Q.M.G., Lieutenant W. H. James, on special service, Major Moysey, Captain Anstey; the 5th Company R.E., officered by Captain Jones, Major Chard, Lieutenants Porter and Commeline; also, Sergeant Wood and six sappers of the 7th Company. It was Sergeant Wood who was wounded.

In the *laager* on the other side of the river were left—Captain D. C. Courtney, Lieutenants Haynes and Main of the 2nd Company, and Lieutenant Macgregor of the C Troop.

The destruction of the king's *kraal* and the severe defeat the Zulus had sustained closed the war, before Sir Garnet Wolseley was able to take any active part in the operations.

The following rewards were granted to Royal Engineer officers for their services in the campaign:—

Colonel Harrison to be a C.B., Major Moysey to be a lieutenant-colonel, Captains B. Blood and W. P. Jones to be majors. Captain Wynne was also promoted to the rank of major, to take effect from April 2nd, 1879.

When the fighting ceased the Engineers were employed in surveying the country, until the troops were gradually withdrawn, and the new political arrangements devised by Sir Garnet allowed to take effect.

ALSO FROM LEONAUR
AVAILABLE IN SOFTCOVER OR HARDCOVER WITH DUST JACKET

THE FALL OF THE MOGHUL EMPIRE OF HINDUSTAN *by H. G. Keene*—By the beginning of the nineteenth century, as British and Indian armies under Lake and Wellesley dominated the scene, a little over half a century of conflict brought the Moghul Empire to its knees.

LADY SALE'S AFGHANISTAN *by Florentia Sale*—An Indomitable Victorian Lady's Account of the Retreat from Kabul During the First Afghan War.

THE CAMPAIGN OF MAGENTA AND SOLFERINO 1859 *by Harold Carmichael Wylly*—The Decisive Conflict for the Unification of Italy.

FRENCH'S CAVALRY CAMPAIGN *by J. G. Maydon*—A Special Correspondent's View of British Army Mounted Troops During the Boer War.

CAVALRY AT WATERLOO *by Sir Evelyn Wood*—British Mounted Troops During the Campaign of 1815.

THE SUBALTERN *by George Robert Gleig*—The Experiences of an Officer of the 85th Light Infantry During the Peninsular War.

NAPOLEON AT BAY, 1814 *by F. Loraine Petre*—The Campaigns to the Fall of the First Empire.

NAPOLEON AND THE CAMPAIGN OF 1806 *by Colonel Vachée*—The Napoleonic Method of Organisation and Command to the Battles of Jena & Auerstädt.

THE COMPLETE ADVENTURES IN THE CONNAUGHT RANGERS *by William Grattan*—The 88th Regiment during the Napoleonic Wars by a Serving Officer.

BUGLER AND OFFICER OF THE RIFLES *by William Green & Harry Smith*—With the 95th (Rifles) during the Peninsular & Waterloo Campaigns of the Napoleonic Wars.

NAPOLEONIC WAR STORIES *by Sir Arthur Quiller-Couch*—Tales of soldiers, spies, battles & sieges from the Peninsular & Waterloo campaigns.

CAPTAIN OF THE 95TH (RIFLES) *by Jonathan Leach*—An officer of Wellington's sharpshooters during the Peninsular, South of France and Waterloo campaigns of the Napoleonic wars.

RIFLEMAN COSTELLO *by Edward Costello*—The adventures of a soldier of the 95th (Rifles) in the Peninsular & Waterloo Campaigns of the Napoleonic wars.

AVAILABLE ONLINE AT **www.leonaur.com**
AND FROM ALL GOOD BOOK STORES

www.ingramcontent.com/pod-product-compliance
Lightning Source LLC
Chambersburg PA
CBHW031632160426
43196CB00006B/379